↑

The Wild Old Man

Poems of Lu Yu

Translated by David M. Gordon

North Point Press · San Francisco · 1984

This book is for Sara Ellen.

buon citarista
fa seguitar lo guizzo della corda

Contents

Introduction

Lu Yu, who with judicious irony called himself *Fang*, "The Wild Old Man," brings to his work the full range of Sung poetry. His poetry falls within three divisions: first, the early period in which the influence of the Kiangsi school—odd, recherché, obscure—was soon replaced by the T'ang giants, Li Po, Tu Fu, and Po Chü-i. The second division is characterized by a strong martial outburst and heroic freedom of style in reaction to the Juchen invasion. In the third division we have the work of his maturity, the greatest number of his more than ten thousand poems. Here, serenity and plainness prevail. We find an old man speaking about absurdly ordinary things of common existence: "Poetry comes to a man when he is no longer thinking about it."

The magnificent mountain passes and forests of Szechwan and the West furnish a persistent landscape for his poetry and are remembered in the title of his collected works: *Chien Nan Shih Kao* (CNSK).

Lu Yu's greatest artistic achievement is the measured or regulated *lü shih* poem, an intricately patterned form in which he could depict any action, thought, or nuance of feeling with unerring precision, control, and grace. His lyricism expresses details so accurately observed that the twentieth-century scientist Joseph Needham regards Lu Yu's writings as an authoritative source for scientific information of the period.

Remarkable in Lu Yu's poetry is the strong tension that seems to develop from deeply rooted opposing forces in the nature of the man himself. We may think of these forces almost as centrifugal and centripetal powers. From Lu Yu's earliest poems until his last we find: (1)

the pull into the unknown—romantic adventure, patriotic wars, and especially the distant central Ho River Plains, which he had never seen; and (2) the pull towards home, fireside, farm, and family, a life of quiet retirement away from the world. It is a haunting paradox, recalling ancient Shun, who, never baffled by antitheses, "grasped both extremes and established the mean" (*Chung Yung*, vi).

The outward pull represents the public Lu Yu, the patriot who carries within him the memory of his birth just as the Juchen Tartars were taking over northern China. This indelible event was nurtured by his father and his own imagination, since Lu was an infant when his family fled before the southward march of the Juchen invaders. This public patriot is the Confucian, would-be statesman, filled with peace plans and war strategies to recover from the Juchens the beloved Ho River Plains of China. Soldier, patriot, statesman, each was a powerful model to action. At any time, in some remote mountain village, sudden rain drumming against his window would instantly become cavalry hooves pounding on the Central Plains in pursuit of the Juchen horses; or the sound of a far-off horn would translate to a bugle call to arms. And yet Lu Yu, patriot and statesman, was a public failure; he repeatedly flunked his civil service exam, and he was dismissed several times from official positions because of drunkenness and ineptitude.

The truth was that Lu Yu had drawn official anger by audaciously trying to stir a very lethargic court into recovering the Ho River Plains from the Juchens. In spite of a certain unrealistic attitude regarding the military capabilities of the Sung army, Lu Yu's disgust with a court policy designed to buy off and appease the enemy was well-founded. (We may recall the nazi occupation of the Sudetenland and think his disgust wholly contemporary.)

He saw political indifference weaken the strength of the people.

But Lu's official disgrace never dampened his determination to save his homeland. His resolution deepened and became a passionate devotion to protect China.

In contrast to the political Lu Yu, there is Lu Yu the rural recluse, whose greatest contentment is found sitting in his kitchen dooryard, ploughing his own field, chatting with his neighbors, and drifting in his small boat, sitting in silence to await the sunrise.

We find these conflicting magnetisms throughout his poetry, and although many of his poems emphasize one or the other, Lu generally holds both aspects in a kind of suspension, as the necessary balance of his being. It is with the juxtaposition of these opposites that he sustains a tension that pervades all of his work. This tension becomes crucial to the syntactic structure of his verse. He reveals on the one hand the imperturbable serenity of life and on the other a transfixing portrait of the evanescence of life. Lu Yu perceives with a spontaneous lyricism the loveliness of life at the very moment that he sees its stark bones rotting in the sand.

Lu's idealism will not compromise either of his visions: the patriot who will save his country or the most humble peasant puttering around his garden.

And yet these conflicting forces do not split his personality. They extend his point of view so that instead of hypnotizing himself with platitudes and self-complacency he remains acutely self-critical, and thus can come to an authentic sense of his own poetic unity.

Thus we see tension as an integral part of his make-up, an insistence on examining both objectively and passionately all the ordinary things that happen to him—even as his body begins to crumble. As extreme age comes upon

him, he continues to encounter and enthusiastically com-
ment upon life, recalling the Anglo-Saxon:*

> Hige sceal þe heardra,   heortre þe cenre,
> mod sceal þe mare,   þe ure mægen lytlað.

And in Lu Yu's ability to maintain a balance between extremes, he has achieved an important human verity that
may compare with the Homeric holding together of opposing and contradictory forces—the outward pull toward otherness and knowledge of the unknown versus
the inward pull toward identity and home. Heraclitus
also sees forces in conflict as the structure of the cosmos.

With paradoxical unity as the basis of his being, Lu Yu
has created a poetry of surpassing resilience, breadth of
feeling, power of utterance, and commitment to the ideals
of humanity.

---

*Michael Alexander, *The Earliest English Poems* (Penguin, 1966) second edition, p. 123: "Courage shall grow keener, clearer the will / the
heart fiercer, as our force faileth."

Biographical Notes*

Lu Yu was born in 1125, in the midst of a turbulent storm, on a boat moored on the Hwai River. A few months later, the Juchen Tartars began marching southward into China. When the Juchens vanquished the Northern Sung dynasty the following year, the court fled south and later established the Southern Sung dynasty with Chao Kou as emperor.

In 1136 (two years before the emperor, seeking peace, moved the Sung capital permanently to Hangchow) the twelve-year-old Lu Yu exhibited unusual literary ability, and because of his father's public service was allowed to prepare for an official post.

In 1141, Ch'in Kuei, a courtier serving the Tartar's cause, forced the emperor to accept an humiliating peace with the Juchens, which cost territory in Shensi, and all territory north of the Hwai River, as well as a yearly tribute. For the rest of his life, Lu Yu remembered this lost territory with nostalgia.

Lu began to work toward his Chin Shin (civil service exam) in 1143, when he was nineteen years old. In 1154, his exam was turned down by the Board of Rites, presided over by Ch'in Kuei.

After the death of Ch'in Kuei in 1158, Lu received an official post in the Ning-te district of Fukien.

In 1162, when the emperor abdicated because of trouble with the appeasement policy towards the Juchen, Lu resigned his post. While still looking for a job, Lu edited a dynastic history (*Hsia Kuo Chu Shu*). The new emperor

---

*Dating follows the Chinese concept of the child already one year old at birth.

Chao Shen began his reign in 1163 and in 1164 noticed Lu's abilities and appointed him to the Privy Council. Later, Lu Yu was transferred to a post in Ching-kou, Kiangsu. When he was forty-one, he left Kiangsu for his family's land in Shanyin to buy a house overlooking Mirror Lake. Later, Lu would return to Mirror Lake to live and write.

In 1169, when Lu was forty-five, he took a job as assistant subprefect of the K'ue-chou Prefecture of Szechwan, and discovered the beauty of the Far West. In 1175, Lu met the famous poet Fan Cheng-ta, who was an officer stationed in the K'ue-chou Prefecture. The meeting was supposed to have been formal, but Lu's informal manner caused him to be teased for his unconventional ways, and thereafter he nicknamed himself *Fang*, "The Wild Old Man."

Lu finished his term of office in Szechwan when he was sixty-four (in 1188) and returned to Shanyin to retire.

Two years later, while Lu was writing "The Nine Songs of the Old Woodcutter," the emperor abdicated in favor of his heir, the weak Chao Tun.

In 1195, while Lu was quietly researching botanical detail in Shanyin, Han T'o-chou, advisor to the court, felt unrewarded for his services and embroiled the emperor and the philosopher Chu Hsi in his machinations.

In 1197 Lu's second wife died. An earlier marriage had ended in divorce because of his mother's disapproval of his first wife. Later, when each had remarried, Lu Yu wrote a poem, "The Hairpin of the Phoenix," in which he agonized over his damaged feelings for the girl, making strong rhymes, "ts'o ts'o ts'o," "wrong, wrong, wrong" ever to have divorced her, with "mo mo mo" for "no no no" to express his resentment that she had so quickly forgotten him. She saw the poem and replied in six words, echoing his same accusation of shallow affection, and soon after died. Lu Yu, at seventy-three, was still deeply affected by the memory of both his wives.

In 1200 Chu Hsi died, and Lu Yu profoundly grieved for the loss of this great philosopher and friend.

In 1204—the same year the Fourth Crusade sacked Constantinople and ended the Roman Empire—Lu Yu sadly watched his sons depart for a disastrous war with the Juchens, planned by the dominating Han T'o-chou. At eighty-two, Lu Yu bewailed his absent sons, recalling Po Chu-i's "father and son affection splintered in five pieces." Lu Yu was rejoined by his family in 1208 when he was eighty-four years old—the war and later peace negotiations had both failed.

In 1210 (some say 1209), Lu died as the dynasty faced the gathering force of the Mongols who would soon obliterate the Sung.

A Note on the Translation

The so-called translator's dilemma of either "literal" or "literary" is false. One simply searches the English resources for maximum accuracy in representing the poet's meaning. Anything less is a halfway house. It may be helpful, but it is not enough.

The regulated verse form which Lu Yu mastered involves a very intricate and delicate patterning of tonal and rhyme sounds with parallel and antithetical couplets. I do not attempt to replicate all of these qualities in English. The *lü shih* regulated verse has eight lines with either five or seven words per line. Lu also liked the *chüeh-chu*, which employs the same qualities as the *lü shih*, but has only four lines. The parallel and antithetical couplets may at times be effectively translated into English.

Here is a paradigm* of the *lü shih*, regulated verse form; it may be doubled for an eight line strophe, and the two first words may be left off for the five word line. If the first line rhymes, five, six, and seven of the first line are changed to "/A − ." L = License (an even or deflected tone may be used); − = the even tone (i.e., the first two tones); / = the deflected tone (i.e., the last two tones):

1	2	3	4	5	6	7	
L	A	L	B	−	A	/	
L	B	L	A	/	B	−	rhyme
L	B	L	A	−	B	/	
L	A	L	B	/	A	−	rhyme

*A. C. Graham and G. B. Downer, "Tone Patterns in Chinese Poetry," *Bulletin of the School of Oriental and African Studies* (London) 26 (1963), p. 1.

While working toward an English equivalent for Lu Yu's line, I found that the caesura divided the Chinese line into an easier to handle rhythmic unit. Lu generally uses the caesura between the second and third words of a five word line, and between the second and third, and between the fourth and fifth words of a seven word line. Thus in the five word line we have two groups of two and three words; and in the seven word line, three groups of two and four words. We may see something analogous to this in Western poetry. For example, the line is the basic unit in Lu Yu's poetry just as it is the basic unit in Homeric poetry. That is, the line must begin with a word-beginning and end with a word-ending, unlike the lyric strophe, where a word may bridge over two lines. And just as the Homeric hexameter is composed of short rhythmic units (cola) with the word-ending occurring in certain common positions in the line, so also the Chinese line is made up of short rhythmic units occurring in certain common positions in the line.

In the Homeric hexameter line, the three most common caesurae are at positions three, five and a half, and eight, which would coincide, *mutatis mutandis*, with the caesurae after the second and fourth words of the Chinese line. The second line of the *Iliad* gives an example of all three of these caesurae:

3		5½		8	
oulomenen / hay		muri / achaiois		/ alge	etheken
baneful / which	many / to the Greeks	/ woes brought			

xviii with which we can compare Lu Yu's use of caesurae in

lang	yen / pu	chü / yü	shu	hsi
wolf	smoke / not	start / feathers	book	rare

from *Remembering How It Used to Be*

These rhythmic units are marked off by caesurae of varying degrees of intensity or subtlety. Thus we can see how the Chinese line is naturally divided according to its shorter units, as for example, the Homeric line was divided by later lyric poets into shorter rhythmic units (the final Sapphic cadence derives from the last cola of the Homeric line). The fairly predictable medial caesural pause in Old English poetry as in "Swa ic mod-sefan / minne scolde" of "The Wanderer" can be found in later poetry: "Lonely men in shirt-sleeves / leaning out of windows" as in Eliot's "Prufrock," and elsewhere. Dealing with the Chinese line in terms of its shorter rhythmic units also entails observing the interplay between word order and rhythmic, syntactical, and conceptual units as they flow together. There can be nothing dogmatic in this formulation.

Just as we can gain some idea of what the T'ang poets must have sounded like by listening to the present-day Cantonese dialect, it seems to me that Lu Yu has filled his ears with end-stopped lines and strong doubled consonants, recalling those dialects native to Western Szechwan.

A Bibliographical Note

At sixty-five Lu, ignoring the effusiveness of his youth, collected his writings in twenty chapters (books). But his early works were rediscovered so that by 1220 his collected works filled eighty-five chapters—nearly ten thousand poems—with the title of *Chien Nan Shih Kao* (abbreviated CNSK).

The following editions have helpful notes and commentary:

Chi Feng, ed., *Lu Fang Weng Shih T'zu* (Hong Kong: 1962). (LU CHI)

Chu Tung-jun, ed., *Lu Yu Hsüan Chi* (Peking: 1962). (LU YU)

Huang I-chih, ed., *Lu Yu Shih* (Taiwan: 1972). (LU HUANG)

T'ang, ed., *Lu Yu Shih Tzu Hsuan Shih* (Hong Kong: 1962). (LU T'ANG)

Other editions containing the complete *Chien Nan Shih Kao* (CNSK) are:

Liu K'o-huan, ed., *Lu Fang Weng Ch'üan Chi* (Taipei: 1970). 6 vols.

Yang Chia-lo, ed., *Lu Fang Weng Ch'üan Chi* (Taipei: 1970). 2 vols.

Some biographical works may be helpful:

Liu Wei-ch'ung, *A Critical Biography, Lu Yu P'ing Ch'üan* (Taiwan: 1966).

T'an Chen-pi, *Chung-kuo Wen Hsüeh Chia Ta Tz'u-tien* (Shanghai: 1961). No. 2516.

Other works which have been very useful are:

Liu, James J. Y., *The Art of Chinese Poetry* (The University of Chicago Press, 1962).

Hawkes, David, *A Little Primer of Tu Fu* (Oxford: The Clarendon Press, 1967).

Watson, Burton, *The Old Man Who Does as He Pleases* (New York: Columbia University Press, 1973).

A Note on the Grouping of the Poems

Since this collection of poems follows the chronology of Lu's life, here are a few subgroupings of the range of his subject matter. The poems are listed by page number:

The Poems

Crossing a Boat-bridge to South Tower

Traveller, midroad, sick,
forsakes landscapes.

Heard tales of South Tower,
might give it a try;

nine-rutted path,
I walk slow where wrath waves rise,

countless hulls, sidelong,
gird the great stream's hub.

Kirk's height, bell and drum
incite dusk and dawn;

hamlet's dooryard of clouds,
from of old till now,

white hair not yet
wiped out my nerve's worth:

wine, play side-blown flute
beneath banyan shade.

CNSK 1.6

Written in 1159 when Lu Yu held a post in Fukien. Age thirty-five.

Saying Good-bye to My Seventh Brother on His Way to Yan-Chou's Army Post

News flashed by border smoke-flares
reached Stone-Head, first;

next, we heard Tartar horse
had ganged-up at Gourd-Isle.

What prince gives ear to grass-
and wood-cutter's plan?

We few clasp farm-field
distress to our chest.

Snow's zeal harries window-board,
our hearts piecemealed—

steep lookout, fix eyes on far,
our linked tears drip:

how today on Hwai-nan road
could one know

chaos of catkins, buds would
drift with your parting boat?

LU CHI 8 CNSK 1.9

Written in 1162. Brother may mean also cousin. Yang-chou is in Kiang-tu district of Kiangsu. Stone-Head is Shih-t'ou, referring to Nanking in Kiangsu. Gourd-Isle is Kua-chou in Kiang-tu district. Huai-nan road in Kiangsu begins at Yang-chou.

Travelling to West Mountain Village

Don't twit this farm kith's
twelfth-month wine, unrefined,

fat year delays guest
with enough fowl, sucking-pig;

hill ridge doubled, lake over rill,
here no road shows.

In willow's shade, bloom shines:
yet one more village—

flute, drum behind me:
spring-altar feast comes soon.

Coat and cap, strict, plain,
old style sustained.

And now we've got
respite to ride the moon—

my walking stick tonight
will tap doors, anytime.

LU CHI 10, CNSK 1.17

Written in 1166 at Shan-yin in Chekiang. "Ride the moon." Walk in the
moonlight. "Tap doors." Drop in for a visit.

At Wu-chang, Uplift

Boundlessly called the dice-play.
That's bootless now.

Sharp chill; snuggled
thin sark, one done-in old man

who only mourns his hair's
matted dried grass,

but doesn't care his living
is blown thistledown.

Smoky rain sullen, dazed
over Cloud Dream Marsh;

slopes and streams, poignant
around Wu-chang Palace.

Heading westward, at each place
I hold back tears,

caress pillow, voice song;
impulse not yet bereft.

LU CHI 12 CNSK 2.24

Lu passed through Wu-chang in I-cheng district of Hupei province. The
gambling game is based on calling the black or white halves of the dice;
here the poet recalls his youth. "Thin sark," a short garment of coarse
cloth. At the downfall of the Han dynasty, Sun Chüan set up the short-
lived Wu dynasty in 229 A.D., reigned as first emperor, and built a palace
in Wu-chang.

Night Mind

Dew jells; peeping
small frogs in grass;

tide wash to settling
geese on sandflat;

gone through years lived
in this lone craft;

nights, I trust in a
traveller's wayhouse.

Ch'ü Marsh, glaucous
without cutoff,

but Pa Mountain,
where is its dark blue?

In all four quarters
a man's job is

to never hate
the homeless wind's drift.

LU CHI 13 CNSK 2.25

Lu wrote this while crossing Hupei. "Small frogs" of autumn are called
"cold frogs." The "wayhouse" refers to the small pavilions set up for
travellers along roads and rivers. "Ch'ü Marsh" alludes to Cloud Dream
Lake in Hupei; "Pa Mountain" to his trips to Szechwan and Shensi
provinces.

Beginning Cold

At boat's stern-post
raw air fills no flag cloth

and along river shore
waste shrine always keeps closed doors;

here, travellers dread tiger,
seldom rise at dawn,

and fishermen with their catch,
as dusk dulls, head home.

The water-shield leaves,
blown backwards, hold last night's rain

amid rush flowers'
soundless play with setting sunfall;

but heart-riven
I hear rapping of the laundry stone:

ninth month of now's year,
still we have not winter wear.

LU HUANG 57.2 CNSK 2.25

"Winter wear" refers to Ode 154 from the Confucian *Book of Odes*.

Pagoda Rock Jetty

Fronting Pagoda Rock
my boat sits thwart-wise;

one window's grain-fire
moon—for whom its white?

Dark crest dwarfs not
year to year's squint qualms,

as my hair abstrusely
greys each day.

The Seven Swamps in far
haze are not of the old state;

but the Nine Songs' grief
bequeaths us its sound.

To dispel tumult:
never without a plan.

Midnight; slack tide;
mind will not settle down.

LU CHI 15 CNSK 2.26

Lu wrote this in his forty-sixth year as he was crossing Pagoda Jetty in
Hupeh, a place celebrated by the poet Ch'ü Yüan (340–278 B.C.). Lu
alludes to the disastrous course the Sung dynasty is following. The
"Seven Swamps" alludes to the feudal state of Ch'u (740–330 B.C.), the
site of the present province of Hupeh. The "Nine Songs" refer to the title
of Ch'ü Yüan's poem.

Crossing East Ju Rapids
into Horse Liver Gulch

A scholar to earn his keep,
with breakneck speed—

high road, path, sheer tricky pass—
bears with what comes.

Aboard in white-water race,
like a wind-borne bird,

I flit by a vertical cliff
like an air-flung ape.

Mouth boasts the far crags,
thousand-layered, blue,

but heart's wit is fixed
on green wave and one punt pole.

Still it beats being the boatsman
who vaults death canyons,

ceaseless, to and fro,
guiding his agile craft.

·LU CHI 16 CNSK 2.29

In the district of Yi-chang of Hupei province, where the Yangtze flows
into the province of Szechwan, the river makes an enormous descent
down the Yellow Cow Canyon; here is East Ju Rapids. A high rock in
the shape of a horse's liver marks a gulch of that name. Lu Yu describes
his descent of the eleventh day of the tenth month, 1170.

Hearing Monkeys

Underfed skin and bones
don't build sound poems;

a lucky day, I'm unquiet,
homeless, downgone;

can know a traveller's insides
by outward drives,

but who could gauge
the quantum of life's ache?

At the Han Border the horn
fades; man wakes;

as Wei-town song ends
traveller must separate.

I have never heard
the grief of monkeys,

like that sound within
the fane of Witch Peak.

LU CHI 17 CNSK 2.31

Lu Yu, on his way to Szechwan from his home in Shanyin, in 1170, passes through Wei-town in Shensi, famous for Wang Wei's poem about a traveller's sadness. "Witch Peak" (Szechwan), shaped like a wizard, has a temple of a female seer; the mountain is known for the sadness of its numerous crying monkeys.

Fair and Clear as I Sit in the Hall

Fish-again town's edged
evening, a pink glow;

things aflower in a way
rid a worn man's rage;

Pa oriole frets, tweets
in sweetwood tree

as plateau stream, soulless,
flows into old palace.

All for homeland? It's ebbed
to anguish for youth's dreams.

Pored over books; many forgot;
ashamed of new work,

and words of firm friend
make it harder to bear.

East to West, cronies—
half have gone under earth's sheath.

LU CHI 19 CNSK 2.33

Lu Yu, forty-seven, in Kwei-chou, Szechwan, is involved in official paperwork for the civil service exams. "East to West" signifies the Eastern capital—Kai-feng in Honan and the Western capital—Lo-yang in Shensi.

At Night Climbing the White Emperor Tower, Thinking of Tu Fu

A mender of mistakes,
white-haired, who misses him?

Down and out, he sang
over all the Twin Streams

and stood on this winged tower
as though here tonight.

Drifts, gyres of the derelict moon,
still unchanged—

upgraded or cashiered?
These things never cease,

but naive or knowing, man's days
have a like deadline.

Headwork brings chill:
whom can I have a word with?

Night's crypt. Gull and egret
lift from sand's edge.

LU CHI 21 CNSK 2.36

Lu, 47, travelling in Kwei-chou, Szechwan, and thinking of Tu Fu who
spent three years in Kwei-chou; the White Emperor Tower is in Kwei-
chou. The poem's title actually refers to Tu Fu as the Small Hill Master,
one of his epithets. "Mender of Mistakes" is the name of a title which
Tu Fu held; "Twin Streams" is a reference to the Szechwan province
where Tu Fu travelled and wrote.

Kwei-chou Chung Yang,
Ninth Day, Ninth Month

At Kwei-chou, drum and horn
at twilight; the hush.

It's just right, the darkened window
as I wake,

thinking earth altar's thick wine
with bruised mum buds.

Dare desire an officer's
berry-tree twig—

peaks, streams trust in beauty;
my farm remote;

but earth, air feel no heart's thought;
traveller's hair thins.

A feast day, and me indoors—
don't laugh my friend,

my being sick,
my silk hat might get blown off.

LU CHI 22 CNSK 2.37

Lu at forty-seven in Kwei-chou has been ill for some forty days. The "berry-tree twig" is a symbol given to an officer of his appointment. Meng Chia (fourth century A.D.) was an officer of Huan Wen's. At a picnic Meng's hat blew off without his noticing; everyone laughed; Meng wrote a reply.

At Fan-chi, a Farm Family

In spring shadows the farm home's
plowing falls short;

from low flat field
bawling of paired yellow bullocks

where mud without clods
fuses into pure ooze;

and a fine rain freckles
shoots just changing green.

These plants divide time
between wind and sunbeam;

mostly there's no need to
draft men to till.

Buying blooms, my
western neighbor wives;

and next door east, with wine
they pledge a new son.

Who says farm folk do not
stay in vogue?

A young unwedded girl
paints chic eyebrows,

her two hands, the candor
of which, unknown.

Whole town emptied
to go watch her reel thread

where farm-hold, kin and clan
delight in the bliss:

not here market's, court's
malign fight and grab.

Always roadward on state's stint—
what's the reward?

Now, three years straight
I've lost the good of my spring plow.

LU CHI 24 CNSK 3.41

Lu Yu wrote this in his forty-eighth year when passing through Szechwan.

At Nan-cheng, Written in the Saddle

Nan-cheng in late spring,
my nag chooses the route;

a city has such snap,
audacity and go,

swagger of willow catkins,
insolent, uppish.

Hauling strings, kids fly kites
that call out, "Bah! Huh!"

Sun downs in a cloud bank
over the old T'ang Fort

but light haze and sweet grass
level on Han altar

since spite never entered
his self-possessed chest.

Eye-reach cuts off where South Peak
slews against sky's lip.

LU CHI 27 CNSK 3.44

Lu at forty-eight in Nan-cheng, which is in the Shieh-cheng district of the southern part of Shensi. The "T'ang Fort" is where a T'ang emperor fled during an uprising. The "Han altar" refers to Han Tsin (d. 196 A.D.), a famous general noted for constant conspiratorial plots against him.

Returning to the Han-chung Border

Cloud's plank-path hung from cliff-edge:
one month's trip;

then horse hooves liked better
the tread of Liang-chou;

joined lands, Chin and Yung;
streams, plains: fertility.

Rivers descend Ching and Yang;
by day, night, glide.

Rest of the Tartars afraid—
why a drawn-out campaign?

A small official's shame is
his private stress,

but a chance like this may
become next year's regret

as the Frontier's crisis repeats
another leaf-fall.

LU CHI 31 CNSK 3.47

In Han-chung, a prefecture in Shensi bordering on Hupei, Lu has com-
piled an official report on the strength of the provinces. He foresees the
ominous outcome of procrastination in dealing with the remaining
enemy forces. "Liang-chou" is one of the old nine-divisions in Shensi.
"Chin" is in Shensi; "Yung" is in Kansu. "Ching" represents Hunan
and Kwansi; "Yang" represents Kiangsu, Chekiang, Anhwei, Fukien.
The "Frontier" is on the border of Shensi contiguous with Pau-ji. "Private stress" refers to himself.

Third Month, Seventeenth Day, at Night, Wine, Wrote This

A few years back,
we ate minced fish on the East Sea;

white-crested billows hill-sized
took some grit.

Last year I shot a tiger,
South Shan tableland, autumn;

that night's return, snow squall
packed my sable robe.

But this year's dashed hopes
could endure a grin:

dappled hair, weathered dark face,
from mirrors I flinch;

who knows, with wine
might still feel like a pup—

shed my bonnet with friends
and whoop it up—

but rebel Mongols unchecked,
heart's not in it.

At bed's head my one sword
jangles its steel—

as flame sweals, dream
of ruined post-house returns;

jabbing window, wind, rain,
on the third watch, pat.

LU CHI 32 CNSK 3.55

In his forty-ninth year Lu was placed in charge of affairs of the provisional government in Szechwan and Shensi.

He shot a tiger on Nan South Mountain between Shensi and Honan. The "East Sea" alludes to Kiangsu province. The third watch is between eleven and one A.M.

Looking from Cloud Tower
in the Evening

Small lookout, east-south,
no one, linger on a song;

here's life's whole span, to fit it
with the world: jagged.

Day's final sunlit patch
immured in a green mist,

perching swallows home
as army horn groans.

Partner of streams, peaks,
man balances the dream;

heart's mind is not the wind and moon,
but who knows?

Word from old pals, cut off
how long by world grime?

Thrice I touch the railing
to tighten thought.

LU CHI 33 CNSK 3.57

Lu at forty-nine in Szechwan and Shensi, pacifying a conquered people
and administering national legal affairs. He was involved in the government of Jia-chou (in the district of Lo-shan of Szechwan). It was at Jia-
chou that he climbed Cloud Tower and later wrote this poem.

Climbing the Litchi Tower

Flat Chiang Stream makes one
with the flowing sky,

and cold in cane window screen,
like sere leaf time;

owner here imagines
me eminent voyager;

not my home ground
but am bound to climb this high house.

Rest on the curved rail,
always forget to pull away;

will descend wobbly stairs,
just wait a little bit—

chief's affairs, little time
for kitchen and wine.

Have not scamped
my job to Jia-land.

LU CHI 34 CNSK 3.57

Lu Yu climbed the Litchi Tower in Jia-chou.

Wine's Midst

Years back, the king was able
to recall my whole name,

but now am haggard-jawed
traveller to hinterland town

in dark coat of the court's
birds in a row;

white hair grown
since I've passed the Sword Frontier,

old garrison's flags
solemn and pale as leaves fade.

On high bulwark
watchman's clack, midnight, moon's glance—

and my will-filled heart
won't yet succumb.

Wined—I hear sandalwood lute's
"Crossin' frontier."

LU CHI 34 CNSK 4.60

Lu Yu in the ninth year of the emperor Hsiao Tsung in 1173. Lu was
forty-nine. He was then acting officer in the governmental affairs of Jia-
chou when he wrote this description of autumn.

Eighth Month, Twenty-second Day, Jia-chou, a Grand Military Review

On the road bows and swords
push out wayfarer

and the riverside's banners
curl up fall wind;

as scribe again
I try on the tight war attire.

Here hill terrain
puffs out the bugle's thrust;

lately Privy Council
can't bear my plans:

these night-going war games,
without shame or sense—

in grasslands,
what feat torturing field rats?

Ought to bend Ho Stream, and
bathe enemy's land.

LU CHI 36 CNSK 4.63

Lu at forty-nine in Jia-chou, witnessing the war maneuvers of autumn, and indicating his anxiousness to move the troops against the Chin invaders.

"The enemy's land" refers specifically to the Lo River and the Sung Mountains, then enemy territory.

Sitting at Dawn

Pillowed, snuggled in quilt,
night's vital pulse I keep.

Muffled, sit dog quiet,
dismiss words from mind;

a potted bloom's strength gone,
without a puff it wilts;

stove's flame in deep ash
comes to dawn, heat alive—

in empty rucksack, now and then,
I hear rats gnaw,

and past small window
one by one, crows wheel.

Can bide time, forget things,
still live a day—

out of bed, I first
open the door to river's edge.

LU CHI 43 CNSK 4.71

During his appointment in Szechwan and Shensi, Lu Yu had little spare time. This poem was written in Jia-chou when he was forty-nine.

After Rain on the Lake

Prairie streams flow into one
then water fields;

Pond, fragrant, after new spate,
flush with the earthwork;

buds hidden by rampant leaves,
in plenty now,

and oriole's soothsay
from high limb: his day-long throat-mood.

Then flowered sleeves and jewelled skirt
urge work aside—

gold cup, kingfisher-green dipper
come to hand's need.

Grizzled head, joy in me,
untamed uplift.

Laugh, fold paper bast
to pen this theme: wine!

LU CHI 44 CNSK 5.77

Written when Lu was fifty, on official work in Szechwan and Shensi; he
had just criticized an imperial plan to pacify the Chen Tartars. His final
hope for recovering China gone, he wrote this while travelling at East
Lake.

East Lake, New Bamboo

Wedge jujube thorns,
wary to weave tight twigged fence;

ripe bamboo's cold blue
reflects riffled stream as

fresh wind ransacks sod,
autumn's first landfall.

A red sun navigates
noon, and you can't know.

You strip the sheath
and hear "suh-suh" "snap-snap";

sprout putting forth, first you see
the clean-cut leaf.

Off-duty, often I'd like
to seek ease here:

head rest, mat, teach me anywhere—
take what comes.

LU CHI 45 CNSK 5.78

Lu Yu, in the summer of his fiftieth year, is in Szechwan describing the
scenery of East Lake; another slice of his roaming days.

Banquet at West Tower

At West Tower carved stones
blazon old heroes

where brocades and played flutes
hover in air.

Miles, ten thousands, unchanged trail,
am die-hard goer

as one year yields, re-
peats last autumn's wind.

Lamp light bends sparkle
on a pearl-lined jacket,

and wine's halo slowly deepens
my cheek's red hue.

Then on the home road: not mind
at all meeting cold.

Above Mo-tzu Lake's midst,
the meticulous moon.

LU CHI 47 CNSK 5.83

Lu wrote this at the end of the summer of his fiftieth year during a
temporary return from Shu-jou to Chengtu in Szechwan. Both West
Tower and Mo-tzu Lake are in Chengtu, Szechwan.

Autumn Thoughts I

Sun's flames, sky's blaze—
how may I sustain?

But friend to me is fall tinge
within wooded park:

cloud's murk, wan sun,
alone; wind's burr, now cold moves;

dew's breath reaches curtain's reeds,
sinks in deep.

My hair falls, dwindles,
follows the dried leaf.

Pained chant, cold wind blends
with washwoman's board's beat—

veering-in geese bring no news
from the Great Plains.

Fingertips on sword. What man
knows his gristly heart?

LU CHI 48 CNSK 5.85

This was written during the fall of Lu's fiftieth year, in Szechwan. Although he is concentrating on the season around him, his attitude towards his invaded country has not changed; he refers to the "Great Plains," the plains of the Ho River Valley which have been seized by the Chin invaders.

Autumn Thoughts II

Western wind blows down leaves,
fills lake's beach;

Attired now in fall-wear,
nothing here but sighs.

Chalky head handles song,
moans over crag-road,

as hushed night, undreamed,
drives upward in mid-sky.

Vague, farfetched,
three rabbit-holes I didn't plan.

Always outcast status;
now what's the point of coin?

To take a wine cup—
no scathe in surplus glee:

rely on strings and flute
to squire year's slide.

LU CHI 48 CNSK 5.86

Lu describes both subjectively and objectively the Szechwan autumn.
"Three rabbit-holes", i.e., if he had not been imprudent he would have
taken more precautions for his future.

Looking at a Map of Changan

For country, I'm grim,
but hair's gone gray-streaked.

From "Mount South" year long
I've surveyed "South Mount,"

and seized spear astride horse
is heart's site—

I scorn these foemen
who moat the town's outskirts.

Sundown's wind lifts
mist above slope's rise; and

leaves down, soldier's cookpot clang
falls from clouds.

In Chin's three parts
fathers give grum reply:

"not seen king's brigades
head for frontier gates."

LU CHI 49 CNSK 5.87

Changan was in the hands of the Juchens at this time. "Mount South"
refers to Szechwan, south of Shensi. "South Mount" refers to the exten-
sive mountain range bordering Shensi province. "Chin's three parts"
refers to Shensi. "Cookpot clang": the soldier's cookpot was used at
night to sound the watch. Written in 1174.

Night Thoughts in Wu

Harvest dark: lift
lampwick to chant Tzu tunes;

old wordsman,
phrase by phrase, does not defraud.

Still might
eye lakes, or climb to steep crag's ledge,

or just dwell
in a small hull's home day after day.

Local wine
can't thaw a traveller's throes,

and hag gives
gaunt forecast of my homecome dawn.

At Pa Bridge,
willows, without bourn, hang in vapor,

but who will break
for the wanderer one sprig?

LU CHI 51 CNSK 5.92

Wu refers to the district of that name in Kiangsu province.
"Tzu tunes" are those famous songs of Ch'ü Yüan which speak of
retiring to a stream bank or to a mountain. Local wine is that from
Szechwan province. "Hag" refers to a soothsayer from the same province. Pa Bridge was a famous bridge near Changan in Shensi, where
willows grew, from which, according to tradition, travellers would ex-
change branches before starting on a long journey. As Lu Yu writes this,
the bridge had been destroyed and the region taken over by the Juchen
invaders; this somber reality colors the poem.

Crossing White Horse Ford, a Recall

My nag shies at his shadow,
nickers,

then abruptly
wades White Horse Ford.

Although this one is not above
Hwang Stream

it skims past things,
still the bitter pain.

At T'ai Hsing's foot
swirls invader's dust;

and Yen south, Chau north,
not a soul, vacant.

Where Yüan and Ts'ao
fought a hundred battles

now these dog-sheep outlaws
stray at large.

LU CHI 52 CNSK 6.94

In 1174, Lu was deputy-governor of Szechwan. White Horse Ford is on
the road from Chengtu, and in crossing, Lu was reminded of another
ford by the same name in Honan, near the Hwang Ho River. He remembers the early Han warriors Yüan Shao (d. 202) and Ts'ao Ts'ao (d. 220).
Yen refers to Hopei's Hsing district; Chau and T'ai Hsing, to Shansi.

On a Tower, Wine, Song

Four ways I've fared
but not yet fulfilled mind's aim;

got up as madman,
dole out medicine in Ch'eng Town.

My big gourd, jam-packed,
goes where need begs,

for infirm age,
to lift 'em out of heartache.

Gourd void, night thought-filled,
I climb this steep pile,

buy wine, roll reed curtain,
bid moon quaff.

Midst cheer I buff sword blade;
emits moon's beam.

Repeat, like lost dog, song's whine;
eyes leak:

to quash war on Chün Heights
and Hsiang Stream,

then cut cinnamon butt
so moon glow again.

Plain man makes plans,
but woe comes like axe blow.

And as for kudos: not yet.
My hair grays.

LU CHI 53 CNSK 6.102

Written in 1175 when Lu was fifty-one. Lu Yu's good friend Fan Ch'eng-ta (Sung poet [1126–1193] whose early work was similar in style to Lu's) sent for Lu Yu to serve him as an advisor. In this poem Lu describes the city of Chengtu in the summer after his return from Fan Ch'eng-ta. Here we see something of his desire to relieve the suffering of the people.

Chün Heights is south of Tung-ti Hu Lake in Yueh-yang district of Hunan province; Hsiang Stream is in Kwangsi province, Hsing-tu district. He refers to Juchen invaders in these two places. He also tells of an old legend about the cinnamon tree that grows on the moon. On the Eighth or Harvest Moon the Moon's Rabbit pounds the Pill of Immortality in his Mortar under the Cinnamon Tree.

Rain

In twilit crosslight begins
as cocoon unthreads,

brushes earth,
then hard arrowheads, airborne.

Through mosquito net light rays
to daybreak-dreams

as the brass stove's sweet grass
steams spring clothes.

Pond fish whip caudal fin
to follow spillway;

over weir swallows zoom, wheel,
touch wings, return.

Petals have only fallen,
not yet blown away,

but wet blooms ruddling bough
are where I put trust.

LU CHI 55 CNSK 7.109

This was written in the spring of 1176 when Lu was fifty-two; at that time he was serving as advisor to his friend the poet Fan Ch'eng-ta.

"Through mosquito net" refers to the "paper tents" (literally) made of fiber, used against insects. They were elegantly painted and impeded light in rainy weather. "The brass stove's sweet grass" refers to fumigating clothes by draping them over a stove that burned incense. The picture is springtime in Chengtu, Szechwan province.

End of Spring

Stone-mirror Peak farewelled me
with late bent shine

at spring's last. I turned back.
So hard to leave.

But slack youth comes to age,
having built no solid base.

Village far, traveller hoards
return's pipe dreams,

yet clover sprouts have overspanned
the turnpike,

with wild turnip blooms
bestrewn throughout the wheat.

Fagged traveller laughs at himself,
battered, luckless—

who'd think I once madly
flew hawk in the hunt?

LU CHI 55 CNSK 7.110

Written in Chengtu, Szechwan province when Lu Yu was fifty-two.
Stone-mirror Peak is a mountain in Chekiang province, Lin-an district
(now Hangchow); its peak reflects light.

Wu-tan East Tower, Long Gaze

Misery at West Window,
of self, one old man;

climbed tower on an impulse
still to be top dog.

Frontier, river, state,
will always rise, fall;

wind and moon clear wine fumes
from poet's head,

spring defunct and with one swoop
all buds void.

By the railing, a standstill:
Do we know or not?

Direct to my home precinct
eye-shot can't reach.

LU CHI 56 CNSK 7.110

This poem was written about the same time as "The End of Spring" (Lu
Chi 55). "Wu-tan East Tower" is on Wu-tan Mountain in the northwest
part of the city of Chengtu of Szechwan province. "Home precinct"
refers to "Wu Tien," the ancient name of Chekiang province, Lu Yu's
home.

Passing a Farm Home, Thoughts

Horse takes reins on riverbank
toward last sun rays;

whose well, grain mill,
and cross-lit unhewn dooryard?

From reed fence dog bays,
spying me pass by;

and on filled frame, hungry
silkworms await fresh leaves.

For ten years I've genially known
these customs;

my home ridge, distant,
tethered to ragged dreams;

oneself plows own field:
hero's taproot found—

grow old, die on South Yang
can't be crime.

LU CHI 58 CNSK 7.114

Lu Yu was attached to the military office of Fan Ch'eng-ta when he was accused of leading a dissolute life. Because of this allegation the authorities immediately had him dismissed from office. Because of his dismissal he wrote more than usual and became even more outspoken in his political views, directly offending the court. This poem deals with the period after his dismissal from office at the end of spring, 1176, in Chengtu, Szechwan. "South Yang" refers to the place in Szechwan where the polymath Chu Ko-liang (181–234) lived as a recluse, plowing his own land.

Out of Sickbed, Jotted Thoughts

Bone-sick, hunchbacked,
I doff my official hat;

lone doer, myriad miles,
traveller on river marge—

lowest job dares not
forget State's grief,

but labor complete,
must still await coffin lid's close.

Sky, earth, spirits,
bond state's shrine and chthonic slab—

capital's old men
crave the king's carriage bells.

One call to arms
would galvanize the past into life;

night's halfway, I turn up the lampwick:
it's still faint.

LU CHI 58 CNSK 7.116

40

Lu Yu's dismissal from his post was a disaster to many of his younger
contemporaries, and the poem alludes to this. After his dismissal the
court adopted a dangerous conciliatory policy toward the enemy.
"King's carriage bells" alludes to the desire by the people to see the ruler
take action. "One call to arms" alludes to a memorial submitted by Chu
Ko-liang of the Shu-Han dynasty, urging the ruler to send out an army
(in 227) against the Kingdom of Wei. "Coffin lid's close" refers to the
scholarly estimate that Lu's work will receive after his death. This poem
was written in early summer, 1176.

At Ho-kiang, an Evening Banquet, Returning by Horseback, I Made This

Midnight, dew downward
imbues green moss;

beyond town, along the river
we began to drink hard,

to drain wine cups fast
as Yellow Ho Stream flows;

my brush splashed ink to phrase
like lathering rain.

Girl's thin fingers, tipsy, I heard
on lyre, quick—

on lampstand, suddenly I saw
flamed candlewick laid waste—

an omen: this epoch
will emptily die.

Astride horse; song abides,
transmit this despair.

LU CHI 59 CNSK 7.117

In the summer of 1176 after he had been dismissed from his official post, he remained in Chengtu. This was written on returning from a night banquet where he seemed to react "dissolutely." He was profoundly disappointed. "Ho-kiang" was a garden southeast of Chengtu, a distance of fifteen li. It was an estate from one of the Five Kingdoms and Ten States Period, Meng-shu, of the tenth century. It had beautiful gardens, orchards, and a tower.

Waking Up

Sleep tastes nice, sweet;
air comes easy through the nose;

blue mosquito net,
flowered mat; the fresh life suits.

Flake of cloud overshoots,
I lose my screen's shade,

and hasteful rain falls:
hear stone talk of tiles.

But pigtailed Tartars still
hold three buffer states—

San Kuan Pass,
ninth sky-troops not yet in the field—

being poet laureate
won't save my bleached head.

I've pulled up a whale—
to do next: now what ?

LU CHI 61 CNSK 7.119

42

"Three buffer states," i.e., those surrounding the capital, Changan. All of these were held by the Juchen Tartars at the time Lu wrote. "Ninth sky-troops" refers to the brilliant military prowess of Chou Yang-fu, a general under the Han emperor, Hsiao Ching-ti, against the Tartars (Hiung Ni) 153 B.C. Here allusion is made to the troops of the Sung emperor.

"Pigtailed" refers to the Juchen hair style.

"San Kuan Pass" in the Pa-ji district of Shensi.

Lu wrote this in 1176 in Ch'eng-ta, troubled by the military events of the day.

Echoing Fan Cheng-ta's "Autumn Impulse"

Sideslip of leaves,
wind-twined Tung tree, now half-stripped,

cicadas cry, I
sense how nigh windowsill is.

All my born days never felt
the cow-blanket blues;

world things pass
like wind in a horse's ears.

Name or pen name
I'm quit of Ten Thousand Pages—

days and nights
now given to the green wine cup—

front door, someone pounding,
wants to find me,

to formalize my new name:
"the wild old man."

LU CHI 62 CNSK 7.123

"Echoing Fan Cheng-ta's," that is, echoing some rhyme words of the poem of Fan Cheng-ta, poet and official.

"Cow-blanket blues" reminds us that Wang-Ching and his wife wept in disgrace because Wang had to sleep on a cow-blanket (incident from Han dynasty).

"Green wine cup" probably describes a green-colored wine.

Lu was in Chengtu and whenever he and his friend Fan Cheng-ta met much wine flowed. Lu was very informal in matters of etiquette between the higher and lower ranked officers, and for this he was criticized and finally dismissed from office. It was from this time that Lu began to call himself "the wild old man." The "Ten Thousand Pages" refers to his frustration with the official paperwork. This poem was written in the autumn of 1176 when Lu was fifty-two years old.

As the Year Darkens: A Feeling

Combat grit for ten years
has darked my war garb

as I've mooned on superb mounts
to cull herbs.

In green days, wrapped in felt
I penned dispatch,

and now, hoisting lance,
still can make lyric.

With wan air's onslaught
autumn climbs the Snake Slope—

wind mutter with winged frost:
we rode into lidded night—

someday we'll file out, brave men
with whom, rapport.

A mirror I don't need
to carp at my decay.

LU CHI 63, LU HUANG 91.2 CNSK 8.125

Written in 1176 at Chengtu in Szechwan.

Frontier Mountain Moon

Cease-fire deemed
decree for fifteen years,

officers without war
idly fend the outpost;

at vermilion doors, deep within,
lilt and dance,

stabled horse fattens, dies;
and bow string snaps.

Fort's lookout, watchman's rattle
goads moon's fall—

thirty years, have borne arms,
now fleece-haired,

flute-tone's inmost, who twigs
staunch man's pith:

sandbank barely
outlines a soldier's bones.

Great Plains' shields, spears—
already we've been informed,

but why let invaders
pass it down to their heirs?

Greybeards will face death
to see it won back—

how many homes tonight
wet with wept tears?

In 1177 when Lu was fifty-three, a peace had been in effect between the
Juchen Tartars and the Sung dynasty for nearly fifteen years. Lu, still in
Chengtu, sighs in regret that the powerful people in court simply sing
and dance and do not prepare for war. They are causing the defeated
Chinese to become accustomed to a shameful way of life.

The title is from an ancient Han song collection, "Heng-chuei" 1.

"Vermilion doors." Rich mansions.

"Stabled horse" etc. Decline from inaction.

"Great Plains" refers to the warfare with the Juchens on the Ho River
Plains. But for more than a decade during the truce the land was simply
given over to the enemy by the court. It was this dishonor which angered
Lu.

Evening Stroll on the River

Side of Myriad Bridge
tied to sun's downset;

facing shore has fish shops
like those on Hsiang's flow.

Crest, trees, I trudge alone—
what regret hold?

Wagons with horse going both ways,
each posthaste;

tall willow, dark in,
I plant my walking stick,

then, flat sand, steadfast,
sit back on Mongol bed:

old chum now at the capital,
no news comes—

how to stay in touch
and share this shade?

LU CHI 71 CNSK 8.135

At Chengtu, written in 1177; Lu was fifty-three. His friend Fan Cheng-ta has been some months at the capital and Lu has heard nothing from him; hence his concern.

"Hsiang's flow" is in Hunan.

"Crest, trees"—out of office, Lu has nothing to worry about.

"Mongol bed" is a kind of portable armchair, made of cotton wadding.

The Way Autumn Feels

In West wind, rife battledores
pound campaign array—

traveller feels border
cares suddenly besiege him;

all beginnings are like this,
for a while.

My hundred years, over half-used,
what now do ?

Crickets in the painted hall
blame the clear night

and at metal well-top
plane tree loses an old bough.

Same pillow in brisk cold,
but sleep doesn't fall:

seek flame, sit to
jot down how words fit autumn's beat.

LU CHI 71 CNSK 8.136

Lu Yu in his fifty-third autumn, at Chengtu; quiet detached mood.

After Hunting, Night Drinking, Telling of Tu Ku

Pale tunic, as snow,
jewelled blade at his belt,

well-wined, mounts metal-trimmed saddle
that outweighs him.

In hidden grass horned falcon
lays bare rabbit hole;

sitting on wind, winged arrows
give sparrow hawk's shrill.

Frontier and Ho Stream—
who'd split them south, north?

Here a self-mastered man
with whom face life or death.

I'll make appeal to the king,
hang it on his high gate—

lampflame, I take my brush:
a tear wets the page.

LU CHI 72 CNSK 8.141

This was written in 1177 when Lu Yu was fifty-three. Lu Yu had made a friend of Tu Ku-tzu when Lu was in Szechwan. He wrote of Tu Ku as "a scholarly man, good at riding and shooting, handles his sword well." Later Tu Ku died; Lu remembered him in many poems. In this instance Lu writes of a hunting trip with Tu Ku, expressing the strength of their friendship.

"Frontier and Ho Stream" alludes to the invasion of the Juchen Tartars. "Frontier" refers to the district of Ling-pao in Honan, and "Ho Stream" to the Hwang Ho River.

Autumn Evening, Climbing the City's North Gate

Wrapped in turban, with goose-foot staff,
on north ramp,

whirled topsoil, west wind
load my eyes with sting,

as wink of signal fire
bruits frontier news.

Two rows of geese circuit
Tu-ling land's autumn—

peaks, streams, gain or fade—
rapt, scratch my pate.

Gist of lived years: peace? war?
I lean on steep wall.

To tilt lance, forge song:
old ways no longer hold—

as wraith, dream
haunts aged land of Liao-chü.

LU CHI 73 CNSK 8.142

Lu Yu at Chengtu in Szechwan, 1177.
  "Tu-ling." The Changan district of Shensi.
  "Liao-chü." An old name for Szechwan.

Autumn Impulse

Ch'engtu town's core,
autumn dark is longsome.

Lampshades' wax leaf
gleams in empty hallway;

in tall plane tree,
moon's white laps magpie on the wing;

and in dead grass
dew wets cries of cold cicadas.

Upstairs, bookman bends to book:
I end.

Try to sleep. But sleep does not come.
Gut knots.

Get up. Walk one hundred rounds.
Sigh hard.

In one night dark hair
turns to third season's hoar frost.

Midplains'
sun and moon use Mongol almanac

and in Yü-chou, chiefs
flaunt our throne's yellow tinge;

rivers: Ying, Ho, Nuan, Lo—
who lives on their shores?

How can you force our elders
to wear felt and fur?

Costly [lamellar] armor,
with eagle feathers at the top—

three-foot sword blades,
with rime-frost snow-glazed steel—

one day crossing the frontier, we
could send out scouts—

at dawn from Paochi—
could reach Changan by sunfall.

LU CHI 74 CNSK 9.142

"Mongol almanac" refers to the lands south of the Huang Ho River ruled by the Juchen Tartars.

"Yü-chou" alludes to the region from Hopei to Liaoning usurping the Chinese imperial color.

"Rivers: Ying, Ho, Nuan, Lo" are all found in the province of Honan, now under Juchen domination.

"Felt and fur" asks the question uppermost in his mind: how can the original natives of this province accept the Juchen rule?

"At dawn from Paochi" reminds us that these two cities in Shensi are 120 miles apart, Paochi on the western border, Changan to the east.

Letting Go

The old authentic men
shrivel up,

and what's to become
of this self's old crock?

Feel dour, use back-scratcher
for sword dance;

wild, tap spittoon
to keep song's beat.

Officials misused
the people's sinew—

at frontiers
fixed peace-deals with Tartars.

Gloss of prestige
unseen in my mirror:

my plans skid,
slipshod; time wastes.

LU CHI 75 CNSK 9.143

Lu Yu, fifty-three, at the beginning of winter in Chengtu, Szechwan.

On Mood

As a kid, had it tough;
nothing held:

wild schemes made,
grieved for human weal;

hunger-knived,
slept on kithless hill

and put together books
with surfeit of words.

Thug Liang gave no thanks
for coddling—

on Kiang's north verge:
mist, mess, murk.

Sent in requests, section:
troop-tactics;

grave things, I fit
each phrase into place.

"As a kid." Lu's family had to flee the invading Juchens when he was still
an infant.

"Thug Liang." Wan Yen-liang was the Juchen chief (d. 1161) who
broke his peace. Liang broke his peace treaty and attempted to invade
the (Kiang River) Yangtze, but was turned back.

"Sent in requests." At the time of Wan Yen-liang's invasion against
the Yangtze, Lu Yu was editor in charge of the military operations board.
His job was to make recommendations, which he did with great care.
He opposed officials who merely wanted to compromise with the Juchens.

Made plea to punish
favored officials

as taproot
of crack-up and morass.

Keen text I told,
but it was scrapped—

my sleeves still
touched with tears and blood.

Now in these past
fifteen years

ragtag Tartars
are gutless ghosts.

Our old, sunk
to button their coats backwards—

hurt like a flame's burn,
how wash this shame?

"These past fifteen years." This refers to 1162, when Lu was thirty-eight.

"Our old." Here Lu mentions the bitterness caused by the Juchens' forcing their customs upon the Chinese people along the Hwang Ho River Plains.

"Button their coats backwards." Literally, from the left instead of the right. The older people found it difficult to accept these changes.

Head's hair in day's span
turns granite,

sick bones,
how long can they hold fast?

Always the dread
old dog and horse

won't live to see
Great Plains regained.

LU CHI 75 CNSK 9.151

"Old dog and horse." Lu refers to himself as still the faithful dog-and-horse minister.

Pillow-Wise

As head rests, third dark
watch sprinkles rain;

to sky's limit
I've ranged all the leagues.

Insect's chirm disdains
dream's charm

as lamp's flicker
mates by-myself mood.

On homeland's behalf,
how hatch a plan?

To quench foe's fire,
mind's heart never abates.

Next year will kindle
the flying general:

again put to proof
on autumn's North Plain.

LU CHI 77 CNSK 9.151

Lu Yu, fifty-three, Chengtu.
    "Third . . . watch." Between 11 P.M. and 1 A.M.
    "Flying general." Li Kuang, a general who had been successful in some seventy battles with the (Hsiung-nu) Tartars, and was feared by them. He was in charge of Yu-Peiping (which I call here "North Plain"), where the enemy was planning an invasion following the autumn.

Rhyming Chi Chang's Poem as Reply

Perched against South Peel's
twelve rails, each in turn,

drawled tunes that tie rooms,
reach back to bleak or blithe days.

Quiet, to recall armed horse,
and balanced lance, grasped—

unused to Ho Stream's freeze.
Our defeat: blame the cold.

To win, lose? Though all's known,
can't control earth's luck.

Right, wrong? At outset
slowly focus inner eye:

Central Plains foiled
the royal army's chief.

How dare we opt out
to some hill grove's ease ?

LU CHI 77 CNSK 9.153

Lu Yu, fifty-three, Chengtu, Szechwan, planning to come out of retirement.

"Rhyming Chi Chang's Poem." Lu is using the rhyme-scheme of Chi Chang's poem as the rhyme-structure for this poem.

"Unused to Ho Stream's freeze." Here Lu refers to the freezing of the Hwang Ho River and the defeat of the Sung dynasty forces because of the cold.

"Central Plains." Refers to the area below the Hwang Ho in Honan.

South Ting Tower,
Meeting Sudden Rain

I've journeyed all Liang-chou
clear to Yi-chou;

en route again this year
crossed Lu River's width.

Flows, many ranged crags,
effort to hold in eye-scope;

and wind, rain, crosswise, lengthways,
rant in the peel-room.

Men speak, mime, chant:
here, fierce-faced Tung tribesmen

and oar-song; heaved wood keens
on downstream Wu scow;

sky's brink stiffens
trekker's inner resistance—

climb aloft to see. Vague:
ahead grief looms.

LU CHI 78 CNSK 10.159

Lu Yu, fifty-four in 1178, still in Szechwan, received summons from the emperor, Hsia Tsung, ordering his return to the East. His appointment to his former post had been cancelled and he had no choice but to return.

"Liang-chou." An old division that includes Szechwan and Shensi.

"Yi-chou." Includes Chengtu district.

"Lu River." A river in Lu district of Szechwan, associated with Han luminary Chu Ko-liang.

"Effort to hold in eye-scope." Here the green of the Lu River meets with the red of the Gold-Sand River where they flow together, with layers of colors.

"Tung tribesmen." An aborigine tribe of the southwest called the Man people.

At Dragon-Joy Shrine
Visiting Tu Fu's Old Residence

On wide plains, grass in chaos:
we've lost the peace.

Guard-tower fires, Tartar grime
reach both capitals.

Among the king's men, the old hand,
his endless miles.

High air gone chill,
now can hear river's chime.

LU CHI 79 CNSK 10.161

Not yet the fourth month and Lu Yu is travelling eastward, descending
rapidly by boat, having reached Chung-chou (a district in Szechwan).
Here is the place the T'ang poet, Tu Fu, once sojourned in 765. Lu Yu
visits the historic site and writes this poem.

"Dragon-Joy Shrine." Lung-shing shrine, eighty kilometers inside
Chung-chou district.

"Wide plains." Again, the area south of the River Hwang Ho in
Honan.

"The old hand." A reference to Tu Fu.

"River's chime." Lu Yu left the following notes: "in fall or winter at
the Shrine [in Chung-chou] you can hear the increased sound of the
river."

Chu City

On broad stream's wall
grass overgrown,
apes, birds, complain;

straight across the other side,
Ch'ü Yüan's shrine.

In one-thousand-five-hundred
years' slack time

steep, fast, white water race
ever brawls over stones.

LU CHI 80 CNSK 10.162

Lu Yu, returning eastward, comes to Kuan-chou in Hopei, and here he
visits the shrine of the famous Warring States poet Ch'ü Yüan (343–298
B.C.) with whom Lu identifies.
   Ch'ü Yüan committed suicide by drowning.

South Tower

A ten-year's while, not held cup
of Wu-chang wine.

Sunlight on rail ledge:
keen regret seeps inside;

boatmen sculling oars,
south and north, pell-mell—

as peaks, streams, thick timberland
wax from the past.

Pay homage to early hero,
but bitter earth in my heart:

steadfast, unbent, alone,
strove on other's behalf.

Propped on stick, burnt-out coal.
Light slants, day browns.

All Tsou's and Wu's miles
unwind a plangent tune.

LU CHI 80 CNSK 10.165

Lu Yu continues eastward and passes through Wu-chang in Hopei on
his way home.
    "Tsou's and Wu's." Tsou refers to the area of Szechwan and Wu to the
poet's home province.

In a Boat Passing Small
Orphan Mountain, How It Felt

Around Small Orphan's slope
sharp sail-wind blows;

again see its fog hair,
as green-blue flame beneath mist-froth;

multi-miled traveller
has passed through Three Gorges' defile;

poem's thousand pages
have cost ten years' pains.

But haven't yet filled
my chopsticks with pallid rush sprouts—

here, first saw a dish heaped
with red diced fish.

To draw a plan for man's life-days—
who cares?

A hemp coat—from here out,
I enter the rain-heavy air.

LU CHI 81 CNSK 10.167

Lu Yu in his sixth month of travelling passes Little Orphan Mountain in
Kiangsi. Lu, in facing his future, thinks of the fisherman's life.
   "Three Gorges." The famous gorges of Kiangsi.

Toward Fukien

Spring's debris you can see
in a small town's flowers;

when snow flies
I'll taste North Villa tea;

don't mind that light, dark
bolt colt-quick past a crack

but alarmed that the cosmos
equals the Ganges' sands.

My fame's on the Mongol frontier—
now heart's youth inane.

This poem's wine cup confronts
hair already flecked;

on king's highway willow sprouts,
plum casts pallor.

Can't stand worn-out nag
and again sky's strand.

LU CHI 82 CNSK 10.172

At fifty-four in the winter of 1178, Lu goes to Fukien to accept a government position in Kien-an. He is thinking that in the past spring he has left Chengtu, and in the winter he has again left his family. His career looks dim. Hair gradually turning white, feeling it.

Going by Night to Stay at Lake-Head Shrine

Carried in sedan chair past
yellow-leaved hamlets,

far bell, damped,
other side of ravine, I hear.

Clean frost for ten miles,
helpmate to the frail moon;

and cutoff geese, half a V,
thread through teased cloud drift.

Departing state, viscera not tough
enough: am reaved.

But for soothing war's moils,
in me spirals spunk's root.

Sy River shore's music stone
responds as of old—

who'll carve there
one brave deed of the Great Plains?

LU CHI 83 CNSK 10.173

Lu wrote this on his way to Fukien when he was quite concerned about
his career.

"In sedan chair." A bamboo chair.

"Sy River." Confucius taught by this river.

"The Great Plains." The plains of the Hwang Ho River, in the hands
of the enemy.

Crossing Spirit-Rock's Three Peaks

On that crag meet horse?
Shocked hell out of old crock.

Shu Range or Wu Crests,
the same washed clean abyss.

From ground up, blue green,
five thousand fathoms:

I'll cram that vast peak
into this flea-sized poem.

LU CHI 84 CNSK 10.174

Written on a trip from Shanyin (Lu's home in Chekiang) to Fukien's
Kien-an. The peak is in Chekiang, in south Chiang-shan district.
    "Shu . . . or Wu." Western or Eastern.

Sleeping Below
Genius Rose-Cloud Ridge

My life, one tuft
of dried-up wind-lapped weed,

been everywhere among men:
road still not worn out.

Just heard at dawn: chickens
from the court's twin lookouts;

again to ride listless horse
through endless hills.

Doubled furs can't withstand
daybreak's frost-grip—

an old tree strives and soughs
in all-night clough gale.

Don't again pursue dreams
of the Western outpost—

ruddy-faced youth years all changed:
young plans vacuumed.

LU CHI 84 CNSK 10.174

Genius Rose-Cloud Ridge is in Kiang-shan of Chekiang province. From Chekiang the mountain enters Fukien's range. Lu, in his fifty-fourth winter, on his way to Fukien, crossed this mountain.

Recalling South Mount

Sable fur, elite steed
were Liang-chou days;

long lance, bill held at ready:
for a lifetime, backbone.

Roused tiger roared in hill-glen,
fought my white blade,

and startled swan beat wings through pass,
outstripped carved bow.

Courtiers toil with tactics
in sleekly oiled tent—

sundown, wine poured, flute-song's tent
has flowers.

Grown old on horseback,
still I'm hale, fit, hard—

when will the king send
squads to allay East Liao?

LU CHI 88 CNSK 11.186

In 1179, during the autumn of his fifty-fifth year at Fukien, Lu remembers the army life of past years in the west. Bored, he recalls a more exciting life.

"South Mount." Refers to Chung-nan Mountain in Shensi.

"Liang-chou." Also a reference to Shensi.

"East Liao." This points to the Juchens.

Recalling the Past

Mind clings to old westward move
that changed my name;

to pursue game for butcher shop
weighed down warriors.

As rain soaks tree, so wine us,
we shrank the sea,

and overwrought as eager hound,
we hymned Mount Hua:

whose heart stands his ground
makes dirge for the old greats.

Now all roads are closed:
I heed my career—

while life breathes, self's smile
is where poem is.

But now to till the plantain:
rain's talk nears.

LU CHI 89 CNSK 11.187

Lu wrote this sometime in his fifty-fifth winter, at Kien-an.

"That changed my name." It was in the west that Lu changed his name to the "Wild Old Man."

"Mount Hua" in Shensi.

On Long Shoal Road

Dusk, passing Long Shoal
Post-horse House

as vale stream finds refuge
in walled brae—

old guy only waits,
stock-still, whistles:

created things
give a poem its say.

Bird companion treeward,
chitchats;

pine hangs,
brushes canyon with boughs.

Sit saddle long while,
slips mind to move on—

it is not
that the horse is inert.

LU CHI 90 CNSK 11.190

Lu at fifty-five at his government post in Kien-an, Fukien. After half a
year he departs and turns back on the road through the beautiful mountains toward Chekiang.

After a Snowstorm, Bitter Cold
on the Jau-fu Road, Some Thoughts

Thawed snow; sundown,
again thickens;

north wind clears,
cold seeks house sills;

piled on furs,
goosebumps rice-sized;

no wine's rounds
would blush my face now,

and fingers could not
curl into grip

since all the long-drawn day
sleeves didn't reach.

Ten years,
tread ten thousand miles—

which way go
without agony?

Hug fire's dint
for a bit,

then take reins,
again feel inner twitch.

I'd hate to not
take care of this job—

for this land's bliss
save the Jade Frontier.

Lu Yu takes a detour by way of Kiangsi back to Chekiang. In Ch'ü-chou
he had written to the emperor Hsiao-Tsung, and received orders to
return to a post in Kiangsi.
   "Jade Frontier." Strategic frontier in Kansu.

A Letter to Ko-leng of Feng-hsin

Fine rain brings cold,
I don traveller's cloak,

go through backlands,
sleep under dew, can't shirk task.

In year's hard times
people eat scant chaff;

officials lax, granary men
are rat-bird bandits,

liberal only with a cane's blows
on human backs.

Don't doom folk to build
border walls, mend bows, swords—

nine fold, the king
has again given decree:

what must be done, is our job,
can't just retire.

LU CHI 92 CNSK 11.214

Lu, fifty-six years old, at Lin-chuan in Kiangsi, sends this poem to a
district official.
  "Nine fold." A decree from the inner palace.

Going at Dawn

River road keeps on
out of reach, horse heads east;

Lin-chuan, homespun dream
again gone hollow.

Sun's lift doesn't yet
dissolve dawn's frost glaze

but wind's brawn's rushed in,
cancelled forenoon's wine flame.

People move toward hill marketplace
after crops failed.

Cast-off life, body old,
always on the road:

Does one just secede to smug
seclusion?

By Bowman Crag,
moored, a sail-rigged fishing skiff.

LU CHI 92 CNSK 11.216

The winter of 1180 was a disaster in Kiangsi with famine widespread.
Lu alleviated suffering by requesting the opening of grain reserves in
Lin-chuan and notifying other districts to do the same. Because of Lu's
notable achievement, Chao Ju-yu, a relative of the emperor who had
appropriated great power, trumped up charges against Lu Yu and had
him fired. This poem is written after Lu received the bad news.

"Bowman Crag" is a mountain in Lu's home in Chekiang (She-te).

At South Hall Watching the Moon

Milky Way lists
across estranged star throngs,

flat on my back,
watch cold moon
visit my window;

then it brought back
the frontier,
once at Liang Chou:

on waking, hard frost
had seized
my body armor.

LU CHI 94 CNSK 13.222

Written in 1181, age fifty-seven, at Shanyin.

The Ninth Month, the Third Day,
Adrift in My Boat on the Lake,
Wrote This

A kid trails along
to grin at the wild old chap,

again I face lake shore,
firm sampan beneath.

Fish mart buyers whelm
the biased sunfall,

chrysanthemum buds in sky's snap
accost new frost,

and overlay of red trees, autumn,
hill; dusk, dun.

Wind buffets dark flag:
altar wine's sweetness, there—

no neighbor refuses
grace of reunion—

for ten years on the road
I've failed the Ninth Day Feast.

LU CHI 95 CNSK 13.225

Written in 1181, when Lu was fifty-seven, at his home in Shanyin on
Mirror Lake.
   "Ninth Day Feast." An important autumn festival.

Book Woe

Today again,
I'm in the glooms,

long while stretched out,
feet pressing wall;

from things' onset
all have a stake in death's fate—

why do you stay
locked in, lips shut?

Autumn wind
on both main highways,

northward, Mongol horse
makes hoof marks;

peace with the Huns,
good battlers kicked out,

inside homeland's pang:
plain tears—

on Ho Stream's Frontier
could go in fast,

loyal, straight men
with guts: wild phalanx.

Afraid I'll be buried
in these foothills—

couldn't seem to get killed
in combat.

To get fame, old,
no era left:

they want no dud
as office candidate.

I lean on ink,
have wielded a lakeful—

core feeling
breaks through my chest bones.

LU CHI 95 CNSK 13.225

In the autumn of 1181 in Shanyin, Lu grumping that he can't be of any use.
   "Both main highways" refers to the north and south capitals.
   "Peace with the Huns" tells about the shameful compromises the Southern Sung dynasty made with the Juchens.
   "On Ho Stream's Frontier" indicates on lands held by the Juchens.

Vegetable Garden

Hundred coins just bought
green rain leaf-coat;

wouldn't want gold-rimmed belt
wrapped ten times around.

Old willow on hill slope,
wind and rain caromed—

who'll sketch me, hoe on
shoulder,
heading home?

LU CHI 96 CNSK 13.230

Lu Yu, the tenth month, 1181, age fifty-seven, in Shanyin, gardening.
   "Gold-rimmed belt" describes an official's dress.
   "Ten times around" exaggerates.

Winter Night Not Sleeping, at Fourth Drum Getting up, Wrote This Piece

Chin and Wu, miles, thousands,
wagon wheel tracks,

often an old village seemed
like a vanished life.

The year's lapse, wine hard by,
carcass gathers age;

in night's gates, pillow rebels,
welter of books;

guttering lamp's flame falls:
from holes rats dash,

dry leaves whish through air,
and local dog lopes past.

Fourscore-year chief
quelled invader's corps—

white-haired, wish to make
something that will survive.

LU CHI 97 CNSK 13.231

Lu Yu at fifty-seven in 1181 at Shanyin.
   "Chin and Wu" refer to the northwest, Szechwan and Shensi, and to the southeast, Kiangsi and Fukien.
   "Fourth Drum" is the night watch from 1 to 3 A.M.
   "Fourscore-year chief" evidently refers to the T'ang dynasty exemplar Li Chi (584–669).

Watering the Garden

As tyro I lugged my one sword,
tramped the whole land.

Final years in tired thorp,
am taught to water seed plot;

past friends withered away,
self, decrepit—

wheels up from entrails:
with whom utter a word?

LU CHI 97 CNSK 13.231

At the beginning of the winter of 1181, Lu Yu wrote this in Shanyin.

Winter Warmth

Twelve-month ends and wind
has driven down no snow;

dust in lungs and liver,
heats, dries traveller;

for ten days have quit wine;
lie in vacant house—

Wu crab, Chin cheese,
just can't bear 'em at a meal.

Each day's strain that the plague
may spread through the people,

and still fear weevils
will scathe last year's wheat;

frost skim and thinned sleet
just not enough—

I breathe deep to ask when
we'll see three winters white.

This old man's mood
fills the land's nine parts:

sit, think back, leading troops
on West Sea's brow,

countless horsemen blow pipes
over snow-filled prairies,

snowflakes whirling against
their black badger fur.

LU CHI 98 CNSK 14.235

Lu Yu describes the winter of 1181 in Shanyin.
    "Wu crab, Chin cheese," as Lu says, cannot be eaten without wine.
    "Three winters white" would be needed to kill the weevils according
to tradition.
    "This old man" is Lu.
    "Nine parts"—an ancient division of the empire.
    "West Sea" refers to the province of Tsinghai.

Sent This to Chu Hsi Yuan-huei, Government Official

Marketplace, desolate
as winter wind—

village jammed
with cold starved hands.

You require folk to share
who've no rice;

tell 'em to buy
who've nothing to pay.

Human stare of hunger, thirst,
barren as the moon—

government mandate:
why stagnate?

Taxes: will you ease
up or not?

Just hold back till
harvest of rice, wheat.

LU CHI 99 CNSK 14.237

In the winter of 1181 (Lu was fifty-seven) Eastern Chekiang was suffering from a great drought and famine. Chu Hsi, the famous Neo-Confu-
cian philosopher, was in charge of the office of disaster relief at that
time, but help was slow in coming. Lu sent Chu Hsi this poem and as a
result the taxes were postponed for two years!

Mourning Autumn

Dead-leaf time lamp
an orphan firefly,

flame glint flares
at door and window;

autumn rain becomes
water clock, and

drops keep up, fall,
dawn to sundown.

Am I like Chu's thrown-
out yeoman

whose banked woe
flowed in stirred words?

With fallen leaf
not dodge locked thought—

kingdom's griefs
reach to inwards.

But they won't let
an old man go to war!

As if door to door,
dunning for taxes

troops are sent
along Yangtze and Hwai streams,

each year
to build garrison towns?

LU CHI 101 CNSK 14.247

In the autumn of 1182, Lu, fifty-eight, writes this poem in Shanyin. Note
the sarcasm here: soldiers are sent not to fight the enemy, but rather to
be fed by the people along the Yangtze and Hwai Rivers.

"Chu's thrown-out yeoman" is the great ancient poet Ch'ü Yüan
(343–289 B.C.), with whom Lu sometimes identifies himself.

"Stirred words" refers to Ch'ü Yüan's famous poem "Encountering
Sorrow."

An Army Song

Yu-Yang boys and girls
poised as flower buds—

spring breeze in tower;
I learn to play the p'i-p'a.

And now must I die
I'd feel no rancor:

am no stranger, this land
made me from scratch.

LU CHI 101 CNSK 14.251

Written in 1183, Lu age fifty-nine, still in Shanyin.

Autumn Affect

White hair, wind's grass,
soon thatch all my head;

back home, three times
I've seen the old peak's autumn.

Wined, lean on high hall,
here sky, earth wed;

sick in middle years,
suns, moons now speed past—

my hundred battles in armor
no help to homeland;

fifth watch, painted horn
only wakes heart's pain.

Bright dawn through foggy rain
on T'ung River bank—

gaze at red maples
as I moor fishing hull.

LU CHI 102 CNSK 15.253

Lu in his fifty-ninth year in Shanyin.
  "Back home" refers to the fact that he has been retired three years.
  "Fifth watch." From 3 to 5 A.M.
  "Painted horn." A decorated horn blown by the watchman.
  "T'ung River" in Chekiang, near his home.

Moon Down

Moon blanches vacant court,
tree shadows fan out;

magpie roosts, unsettled,
interweaves boughs, on wing;

Gramp seeks to be naive
as small boy or girl—

managed to touch stream of fireflies.
Dew wets sleeve.

LU CHI 103 **CNSK** 15.260

Lu Yu in 1183 in Shanyin.

On an Intercalary Month, Third Night, Staying Westward to Watch New Moon

All my lived life the third
day moon enthralled me—

might be as in a filled pool
dipping a jade barb.

Weighed with years in this world,
yester friends few—

one drink of wine—with whom
discuss life's ordeals?

LU CHI 104 CNSK 16.273

Lu Yu in the winter of 1183 in Shanyin.

A Drink in the Fields

Dark Mountain's millennium
of tough old strugglers,

unstrained wine, three cups:
I'm free of life's straits.

I prowl the ruined past, toppled
walls, moats, effaced,

seeking friends anywhere—
butchers, vendors of broth.

Level field gives way
to green of spring's weeds;

fine waves, far off, somersault
in sun's red after-fall.

My ailing years
I confide to sky and earth—

riding a cow, play flute,
in tune with village boy.

LU CHI 109 CNSK 17.289

Lu in 1184 at sixty. "Dark Mountain" is in Shanyin.

Drinking Song (fragment)

....

though mind knows what is
and is not

mouth cannot
simply submit.

For now, I'm aged,
my health unwhole,

head turning bald,
my teeth fall out,

but I look at sky
breathe relief—

underfed,
never happier.

Firm heart underearth,
but rots not—

a thousand years,
it can still resurge.

Lu Yu in 1190 in Shanyin.

Hill Garden

Bought this new garden patch
near fish-catch rock;

right off, put up a grass roof,
framed the rough door.

High bluff gone through a dusk
rain that's rinsed its brow

and flowers lean on ductile wind
that gives them wings.

Current events only frighten
my old eyes

and wine, in a word, brings me
to pawn my spring wear;

but my wild songs, when I'm soused,
sir—don't smile—

will dissolve a hundred feet
of Grief-City's wall.

LU CHI 125 CNSK 22.375

Lu at the age of sixty-seven in 1191 in Shanyin. His life was eased by a
government pension he received about this time.

"Will dissolve." Cf. *d'enuo gandres*, "Warder from annoyance," in
James Wilhelm, *The Poetry of Arnaut* (New York & London: Garland
Publishing, Inc., 1981), pp. 54–55.

"Grief-City" is a metaphor.

Cloud Gate, Sitting Alone

Mountain peaks north, south,
nowhere not been.

I look back on sixty-
seven Cold Bright Days,

and now I'm age-buckled,
shaky-footed gait.

Alone, sit, burn incense.
Hear stream's tone.

LU CHI 125 CNSK 22.378

1191, Lu, aged sixty-seven, at Cloud Gate Monastery in the poet's home district.

"Cold Bright Days." Easter.

How It Feels to Write

Too old.
I'm dead now any day.

To achieve something—
self still hopes.

Clear leaf flutes
on T'ai Peak Road—

what day will the king
send out troops?

LU CHI 125 CNSK 22.383

Lu in 1191 at sixty-seven, in Shanyin.
    "T'ai Peak Road" refers to a mountain road in Honan occupied by the Juchens.

Winter Night Reading a Book
and Suddenly Hearing a Rooster Crow

Petty filth: gossip grin
of senile men—

man who wins not in the world
turns, plows own field.

On sky's ring, I'm bound
to moon's many-leagued room;

as lamp lights my book's page
barn fowl crows:

my career wiped out,
I keep to myself—

by and by half-baked sneaks
will have all the fame.

Rank spring grass overgrows
how many brave men's bones—

my white hairs' arid scrub:
no use getting upset.

LU CHI 127 CNSK 24.399

Lu Yu in the winter of 1191, in Shanyin.

Adrift

Drifts as ghost on stream, cove,
threescore-ten man

wants to kidnap one laugh.
Who will join him?

Wind sole friend. Snow-haired,
hardships hoard my age;

in quiet, my weed gate
hides the bare cupboard,

but the polished phrase, still
from my resilient pillow,

and inner drive at times
depends on the tower.

But as to praise or blame
of men—who will be blunt?

Those whose bones have rotted
will tell you what's what.

LU CHI 129 CNSK 24.402

Lu Yu in the spring of 1192, age sixty-eight, in Shanyin.

At Night Sitting Beside a Stream

"Small room" stars upright—
"heart" stars cockeyed—

North dipper tends straight up,
south dipper sinks down;

in smartweed roots, will-o'-th'-wisp,
there firefly blinks,

in knotted reed brake,
bird's grief: "sister's hate" sighs.

I ease back in old army chair
past the third watch,

and creekbed wind puffs my shirt;
moon as yet without vim.

Jade Gate Frontier—
Touch-Clouds-Town—

When will the outposts
fly our dynasty's flag—

since white-haired bookworm
can never forget its weight:

no corpse yet, I'll make you
behold our "Great Peace."

Written in the summer of 1192, Lu in Shanyin, age sixty-eight.
   " 'Small room' stars." A constellation in Scorpio.
   " 'Heart' stars." Antares.
   "North dipper." Ursa Major.
   "South dipper." Sagittarius.
   " 'Sister's hate.' " A bird with that name.
   "Jade Gate Frontier." A frontier in Kansu.
   "Touch-Clouds-Town" is in Suiyuan Province.
   Note satiric treatment of "Our Great Peace."

In My Nest of Books
on a Winter's Night Waiting for Dawn

Swept leaves jam stairway.
Cold hound loiters close;

in grass-weaved fast-staked coop
old rooster crows,

and wind and frost thrust the year
inchmeal toward fag end

as shape and shadow depend
on lamp flames' fulgence.

Thousand years' history
pays homage to a man's deeds:

from frontier, river, long miles,
I rue my career.

And I'll cling hard till death
to chronic regret—

aged, ill—how can
I still re-enlist?

LU CHI 135 CNSK 26.426

Lu at sixty-seven, 1192, Shanyin.
   "Rue my career" indicates Lu is still troubled by his loss of position
when he was stationed at Kiangsi in his fifties.

Autumn Sundown, Leisure, a Stroll, at a Neighbor's Place Where I Have Been Recently Laid Up, All Happy and Welcome

Wild gaffer, revived,
heads out for a ramble;

weaving girl peeks through
screen to meet herdboy.

Wine, full bodied,
know earth-altar feast is about;

and wheat flour's huge round cake
cheers harvest home.

Am back to first insight,
good built-in at man's birth:

looking at these folk,
world events don't have much heft—

vermilion trees, blue mountains
like yesterday—

at Changan, honored, dismissed—
how many men?

LU CHI 140 CNSK 27.446

Lu Yu in 1193, age sixty-nine, in Shanyin.

Rain and Night

In year's dusk thatched hut
is tough to endure;

teeth dangle, soon to fall;
where hair is, soon bald,

but heart's wit scours miles
past Big Stream's frontier.

Self's frame lies by
only window's blown rain;

doctor not reached:
one just puts up with pain—

books, can still read
enough to forget need's squeeze.

Night, late, waking,
a cricket gossips at my side—

then I saw the lampwick
shatter in damask chips.

LU CHI 141 CNSK 27.446

Lu Yu in the autumn of 1193 at Shanyin.
  "Big Stream." Hwang Ho.

Deep Breath

Pent up sigh, doubled,
held in breath,

with whom can I
turn back a man's time

as twilight shadows
press life's footsteps?

Know only: old-timers
thin out like hair.

Evade disaster,
but when it comes back, trapped.

Bit by backbite:
brood shut-mouthed? No!

This year dearth's pierced
through bedrock—

had hoped to buy old jetty
to catch fish.

LU CHI 146 CNSK 30.475

Written in the summer of 1194, Lu in Shanyin.

Poor and Sick

Gone through seventy years,
but still do with a hoe;

harried, broke, wearing
youthhood's white hemp.

Kind deeds: neighbor priest
on the go, gives me rice,

hermit friend from deep gorge
drops by with a fish,

and an unknown gent comes
to the wall-head fetching wine.

Wake from sleep—breathing while,
take a high-shelved book:

must know both sleek and shrunk times
to avoid jolt—

in my chest, unfenced expanse—
scope, breadth.

LU CHI 146 CNSK 30.480

Autumn of 1194, Lu in Shanyin.
   "White hemp" refers to his youth before public employment.

Autumn Evening

Anew, tamp down threshing-floor
flat as a mirror's face;

kinsfolk, family, have glee
getting in fall crops;

old guys come, lazy bones,
abashed by robust young—

sweet to drowse as I hear
rice-hulling hammer tap.

LU CHI 147 CNSK 30.480

Written in autumn of 1194 in Shanyin.

In My Study, Bright and Warm, All Day Sitting. Getting Tired, with My Cane I Walked Out into the Garden for This Amusement.

Balmy doze fits human frame,
outdoes backrub—

Kiang Stream south, tenth month,
mellow air still holds,

and doubled reed screen, not
rolled up, keeps sweet long;

old inkstone, bit bowl-shaped,
gathered much black.

Moon's up, run to see
how plum casts its phantom

as wind's thrum convoys
the din of touring geese.

One cup of plain stuff, sir,
unbends, ups lip-ends—

on the cow's back I tap
her horns, chant refrain.

LU CHI 147 CNSK 31.487

Written in early winter 1194, Lu, seventy, in Shanyin.
   By tapping on a cow's horns and singing, Ning Chi got the attention of the Duke Huan of Chi, thus obtaining a post with him. This was during Spring and Autumn times.

Eleventh Month, Fifth Day,
Midnight, Happened to Write This

In river town's grass lane
man's tracks languish;

one, white-haired, laid up sick,
who lives for words.

Window space where moon moves, I
glimpse plum's mirage

as, head pillowed, wine's high gone,
geese cronk hovers at ear.

Shut out of world, sweet
to me, thousand old smiles:

rode fast, ever strove for peace
on both River banks—

what future man will
recall that past year's feat:

as I nagged the king with tears
to dispatch troops north.

LU CHI 148 CNSK 31.492

Lu Yu in 1194 in Shanyin.
  "Both River banks." Hwang Ho River.

New Spring

I'm at age's rim:
three years ill,

and new king's first
ten days overcast;

drooping fence,
a dried vine ties up,

and ruined wall
overrun with green moss.

Grief for own land,
labor, alone, tears—

to lull Huns,
warrior bends heart's will.

I'm disjoined from my
kids' world—

how make them
a hoar-headed song?

LU CHI 148 CNSK 31.497

Kuang Tsung abdicates to his son Ning Tsung in 1195; Lu Yu, seventy-one, in Shanyin.

Roadside Song

Cold rice mixed
with sandy grit,

short coat fronts
frost-clotted dew,

and yellow leaves fill
post-house yard

as government man
astride ass ambles off.

Heading south-north
on great highway

carriage wheels without
cease in sun's hours.

Do those bigwigs have
all the brains—

me alone foodless
till nightfall?

Chill nips me at
roadside, as I sing,

with purple-gate
people unaware;

autumn, crossroad,
ash leaves cascade—

anguish, like an
axe-blade, now.

LU CHI 150 CNSK 33.510

111

Written in the summer of 1195, Lu, age seventy-one, in Shanyin.
  "Purple-gate people." Those with court connections.

Recall the Old

Called back old days:
clothed light, walked untold leagues,

packet-boat, post-house,
not to speak of thoroughfares;

trod what's left of cliff-hung
planks, burned by Han Ti,

stayed with T'ang family,
at Snow-Peak, outside town.

Soldier's aimed heart
still feeds yesterday's dreams,

but as years fail, remains
only to plough, come spring—

at west window abruptly hear
rain climb stair-wise.

No one. Me. By lamplight.
Not quite serene.

LU CHI 155 CNSK 34.522

Written in 1195 at Shanyin.
   "Han Ti" refers to the first Han Emperor, Liu, who burned the cliff-plank road in the high mountain passes.
   "Snow-Peak" is Snow Mountain in Szechwan.

Remembering How It Used to Be

Wolf dung smoke didn't rise;
feathered dispatch rare;

from headquarters they'd
ride out at dawn
to drive game;

and the road came down
to the foot
of Mount Ting Chün,

where windblown
red leaves filled
a body armor shell.

LU CHI 157, LU CHU 131, CNSK 34.527

Lu Yu in Shanyin, aged seventy-two, recalls the undisciplined army after
its conciliation with the Juchens.

"Wolf dung" was used for smoke signals.

"Feathered dispatch." Attached feather indicated emergency.

"Ting Chün" is in Shensi.

How It Is

Wind's stern throat,
autumn's first thistledown—

crook-boned dragon,
I've not yet expired.

Not only this day
am I old

but spent whole life span
on the edge of want;

eating herbs, greens,
as a kid, gaunt, lean—

at frontier gates
they used to jeer.

But in this world,
one mind persists:

on Ho, Luo Banks,
invaders' dust still flies.

LU CHI 159 CNSK 35.536

Written in the autumn of 1196, Lu age seventy-two, in Shanyin.
  "Crook-boned dragon" describes the conditions of his old age.
  "Ho, Luo Banks" are the Hwang Ho River in Honan, and the Luo
River in Szechwan, an allusion to the takeover of the Juchen Tartars.

In Anger

Steel-gray, failing,
I'm supine in swamp's midst,

lean against sky-earth,
bring to mind lone candor:

seized by great want,
Su Wu for food ate felt.

In savage grief, Chang Hsün
ground his teeth to stumps.

With subtle rain, spring weeds
overrun shrubs and gardens;

crumbled wall's night moon,
in Lo Yang Palace—

proved heart does not buckle
with passing years:

dead, under clay, yet ghost
still potent with courage.

LU CHI 163 CNSK 35.547

Written in the spring of 1197, Lu at seventy-three in Shanyin. Lu Yu lost his wife in the fifth month of this year.

"Swamp." Mirror Lake in Shanyin.

"Su Wu" was an exceptionally brave soldier against the Northern Tribes, Han dynasty, 143–60 B.C.

"Chang Hsün" (709–757) died fighting against the An Lu-shan rebellion.

"Lo Yang Palace." The scene of the rebellion.

Late Spring

Routine lull under rush roof
on Glass Lake shore:

but gathering countless books
pinches flat purse;

swallows leave, return,
again squander day;

buds open, petals fall,
then we've traversed spring.

Open book, ecstatic
to see whole life's friend.

Pond-shadow alarms
don't ripple an old pro—

smile inside, clear out Huns:
there's where heart is—

seeing what needs to be done:
will risk what life's left.

LU CHI 164 CNSK 35.548

Written in 1197 in Shanyin; Lu, seventy-three.

Sickness, at Night, Composing

Stranger like a sick crane,
sinks down, up again;

and lampwick's waif firefly
hides, then unfolds;

clover blossom urged on,
spring seed sown,

as plane tree leaves bring
sound of on-the-way-rain.

Rivers: Jung, Ho, Wen, Lo—
when get 'em back?

Straight minds, well-willed men,
in vain blame selves:

only must face Hun dust:
one dawn would clear it—

these bones won't mind final
bed among bitter field-weeds.

LU CHI 164 CNSK 36.549

Written in the summer of 1197, Lu aged seventy-three, in Shanyin.
  "Hun dust." His mind is always on recovery of the lands invaded by
the Juchens.

Remembering Past Times

Thinking old days, warfare,
along Hwai shores,

bowls of cheer, for us horsed;
for us folk spilled tears;

night rest on high tombs to
forecast from stars' contours;

dawn, to climb wagon lookout
to spot hostile dust.

Common road to kudos:
for him who endures.

Who'd have guessed, to be old,
ill, just moping around—

lamplight near, I flip
through pages—tears:

how many men today miss
the mark of their heart's aim?

LU CHI 165 CNSK 36.557

Written in 1197, Lu age of seventy-three, in Shanyin.

Deep Breath

In just-fledged years, from the first,
never pined for pelf,

kept only one mind:
to do deed for man's behoof.

Hoar-haired, no chance
to test peace plan on War Tribes—

as plain man, face stream and lake,
go through this life.

Who lives for books,
true, frank, wants to converse?

Bones rot, but am still stirred
by kept-alive heart's-rote:

Stone Base in Ho's flow
to Jang Peak's genius in sun flash—

to die first? Helpless eye-glare,
to never see our Great Plains.

LU CHI 166 CNSK 37.573

Written in 1198, Lu, seventy-four, in Shanyin.
   "Stone Base" and "Jang Peak's genius" refer to mountains in Shansi
and Shensi. "Great Plains" refers to the banks of Hwang Ho.

Harvest Chant

On wall's head
fold and twine
of persimmon's gold,

and kinsmen with
just-reaped spikes
vie for threshing floor;

the helved mallet
husks pearls,
sparkling the ground

as the cauldron,
steaming jade,
joins all with its sweet.

Crowds of men
in a block
haul grain to state bins

so that the clerk's
roast jells;
no time to taste.

Each man's tax paid,
they bolt
with the glee of whelps;

liquored,
they cradle together
along thoroughfares.

Then, a few years,
this kith
fell into famine's jaw;

they'd sag
in a ditch;
starve; fixed eyes swapped death's stare.

Then cops,
reeves, roamed
like voracious wolves;

a woman,
corpse-stunned:
her son stiffened into dust.

How know
if the steel sky
will give bearded sheaves?

If ridge
bear its measure,
rich land teem cartloads?

I yearn for
rural lane
to lay up and store,

hold back on clothes,
ease up on eats,
sweat over mulberries,

with the hindsight
of eating without sate
dregs and chaff—

and don't hatch
the flood-drought griefs
of Yao and T'ang.

LU CHI 167 CNSK 37.575

Written in 1198 in Shanyin.
   "Yao and T'ang" are archetypal emperors.

At Three Mountain's Pear Gate Made This

Me as tot, could
barely toddle, met woe—

my folks on Mid-Plains,
fed up with running like rats;

along Hwai's shore one night,
heard thug's horse neigh:

jumped, fled, not wait
for barn fowl to call at dawn;

hid wheat loaf in shirt,
slunk flat under grass—

on the run many times
ten days no steamed rice. . . .

LU CHI 168 CNSK 38.585

Written in 1198, Lu seventy-four, in Shanyin. A memory of Lu Yu's
childhood as his family was fleeing the invading Juchens.
   "Three Mountain's Pear Gate" in Shanyin.
   "Hwai's shore" refers to their home in Kaifeng.

Blissful Rain Song

*It rains no round
pearls, nor smooth jade,*

sixth month pours down rain
and it rains pure grain.

Ten years' flood and drought,
our food, half-beans:

people chopped down berry,
then leaf tree, sold buff calf;

past year's sparse harvest:
food enough to scrape by,

but now this year
we'll learn to loathe wine and meat.

Drink and food filled, now
to go back and mourn

those not seeing the rice
head up into ripe ears.

LU CHI 171 CNSK 39.603

Written in the summer of 1199 in Shanyin.
    "Berry" and "leaf" for silkworms.
    The poem is introduced by a different metric line.

East Village

Farm people care for me
as I chance on their path;

pour a cup, get right around,
pay little visits.

After a stop, take basket,
pick out green sprouts;

before gate front, call in
to buy some small pears.

LU CHI 172 CNSK 41.622

125

Written in winter of 1199 in Shanyin. Lu was seventy-five.

On a Cold Night Pillow

House ages, frost numbs,
and sleep does not nod;

aloof, a waterclock stroke
has slipped the third watch.

Crow's caw in timbershade:
the moon's tip buoys up;

dog gnars from the shore
at a night-gliding junk.

And marketplace singers—
you feel their harvest zest;

sweet voiced without war drum,
they bask in the peace.

Want to write these words
but too sluggish to budge,

lie flat, rapt in the drab lamp's
lurk and flash.

LU HUANG 137.2 CNSK 44.663

"Third watch." 11 P.M. to 1 A.M.

Crossed-beamed Gate

Bowed lane, crossed-beamed door,
low stubby fence;

ash tree, catalpa shade,
lean on tough cane staff:

to me, dotard, today's manners
don't delight eye—

heart only reaches for steep
peak's azure that ever was.

LU CHI 175 CNSK 46.678

Summer of 1201, Lu Yu at Shanyin age seventy-seven.
   "Crossed-beamed Gate" alludes to Ode 138 from the Confucian
Book of Odes.

Hearing Horn

Great white star-river,
silver, sky pale blue;

far horn brays:
suddenly before me, Jade Frontier.

Back, years, I knew with age comes
berry, hemp, farmstead:

deplore the loss of Ansi's
limitless leagues.

LU CHI 176 CNSK 47.689

Lu Yu at seventy-seven in 1201, in Shanyin.
  "Star-river." The Milky Way.
  "Jade Frontier." A pass along the northwestern border of China.
  "Ansi." A place in Kansu.

Taking a Trip, Returning to Anchor at Lake-Bridge, Made This

West Shu, East Wu,
been through the dust, travelled;

thousands of cliffs, steep chasms,
right here, home district.

Short sailcloth wafts moon
over Maid Stream, nightwise;

by small ass to seek a poem,
Yu Shrine, dead-leaf time—

village wine on credit
all you can hold—

backwoodsman fired up
to help us find the path.

How attain the way Wang
handles words,

or makes painting of Lake-Bridge,
tinged with autumn's flame.

LU CHI 177 CNSK 48.705

Written in autumn of 1201, Lu seventy-seven, in Shanyin.
   "West Shu." Szechwan.
   "East Wu." His travels in Fukien, Kiangsi, Chekiang, etc.
   "Maid Stream." A river in Chekiang.
   "Wang." The T'ang dynasty poet-painter, Wang Wei.

Unsleeping

At high lookout, hear all
night's watch, short and long;

uncanny dream without grounds,
could not resolve,

chill rain trickled, as if
drops dripped on my heart.

Sole lamp flame, sideways
toward pillow edge, brightens;

read book you can taste;
flesh, bones forget age.

To pay back homeland
I have no hope; tears flow—

hazard all with these wilted limbs
in futile death—

but first, gave neighbor my word
I'd plow his spring field.

LU CHI 178 CNSK 48.706

Written in early winter of 1201, Lu seventy-seven, at Shanyin.

With Evening

Chopping taros
I shoulder them on a pole
for a broth;

the snowed eaves
quit their drip;
as sun darks, chill grows.

Unbaffled
by the whole blank day
as no guest drops by,

often from
the lapsed orchard sounds
axe clink on a tree.

LU HUANG 176.2 CNSK 49.723

Going by Boat
on Chien Stream to Ko Bridge

Over a year I'd dreamed,
thought of Hui-chi town;

glad to hoist high sail,
eager prow through wave.

To East-West hadn't seen
Twin White Pagodas:

first sailed Chien Stream,
south-north, shops on each shore.

Young boys drummed and piped
to greet my return boat—

old gaffers with wine cups give
gossip since I left.

I think of my hut how
night not yet has come—

bamboo patch just seen,
sunset spreads, glow pours.

LU CHI 184 CNSK 53.773

Written in 1203 when Lu Yu was in Linan (in Chekiang).
  "Chien Stream" and "Ko Bridge" are near his home.
  "Hui-chi town" is near Shanyin.
  "Twin White Pagodas" refers to a mountain in Shanyin.

On the Lake,
Returning at Nightfall

Crowding the mirror with fresh frost:
how cope with age?

In small straked punt
each day tans my face with wine;

a game, like running cottontail
with yellow hound,

forthright as flag troops,
winding up the White Wave War.

Freeze nears the tansy blooms;
still hasn't taken hold,

and in rain's glut, oranges
just roll supplely in hand grip.

Then by the lake's mulberries,
in the mart, people

elbow to see me, old hillsman,
pound oar and chant.

LU HUANG 144.2 CNSK 54.784

"White Wave War" is an early war with the Tartars in later Han times.

Seeing Off a Stranger

Traveller visits.
Paired cups fill;

wined, chant, skyward,
soared to sapphire;

we sat, out of time,
till empty bellies growled—

deep-toned like
a turning wain wheel.

Quick-fried chestnuts,
with baked taro roots

tasted so fine,
vied with bear's paw.

Once filled, hundredfold
worries vanish:

hands, tongues talked
of Shi-Shiuan.

Fagged out, stranger
bade farewell;

held lampflame,
saw him out rough-hewn gate:

among trees,
birds pitter awake—

dipping moon,
diagonal gold dish.

LU CHI 187 CNSK 56.804

Written in the winter of 1203, Lu seventy-nine, in Shanyin.
"Shi-Shiuan" are two ancient emperors.

Bird Songs

"Cloth-grain, cloth-grain":
   dayspring not yet full glow;

"urge-till, urge-till":
   man's up, ploughshare in turf.

Job on the road no joy
   as field-folk own—

eastward sweat, to the west
   all done: how life's met.

LU CHI 195 CNSK 66.927

Written in 1206 in Shanyin. Lu was eighty-two.

Out of Sleep

Wake from sleep: my bearings lost.
Wave slow fan.

Impress of face on pillow
fades not yet.

Slope's red tinge and rock
bamboo, run to waste—

lone butterfly strays my
way—mateless, remote.

LU CHI 196 CNSK 67.934

Summer of 1206 in Shanyin. Lu was eighty-two.

A Boat Ride
to Gold-Home-Path Village

Old, can't go back
to tend field crops, berry trees,

but to count hens and pigs
I don't forget.

Wash my feet, crawl into bed:
here's heart's release—

grandson new grown everyday,
now knows how to cook soup.

LU CHI 198 CNSK 69.966

Written in the winter of 1206, Lu at eighty-two in Shanyin.

Spring Evening:
Just the Way Things Are

Fishing town, wood cutter's yard
at spring's butt-end;

eighty-three years old:
sick bones, bare joints.

Done down Huns, ghosts on the run:
my sprouts thirst for rain—

close the door: grieve for state
and weep for the people.

LU CHI 198 CNSK 70.981

Written in 1207 in Shanyin. Lu is eighty-three.

Early Clear

Aged, unsound,
always crave shut-eye;

wind drone, no one.
Worn out with rain's din.

Wheeling, light-winged,
paired crow, magpie

means new air shines
aloft, clean-cut.

LU CHI 199 CNSK 71.989

140

Early summer of 1207.

Going Out in the Rain
to Look Around I Wrote This

Abrupt rain already
roils down the eaves,

as bracing air tang
slips through the bamboo door.

This year unbars my ninth ten
and still not dead;

to sit by my notebook,
never fed up.

We laugh at the wise and the naive
since we're half of each,

but it's tough when you're gripped
poor and sick in one same clutch;

enraptured by a plum tree they say
stops thirst:

might stroll down the road,
scrutinize a wine flag.

LU HUANG 151.2 CNSK 71.990

Spring Ramble

On the road to Orchid Inn
changed to spring clothes;

on the flank of Plum Shop Bridge
followed sunfall's tilt.

Rife adage says the stream's
daimon is an old man?

My light boat, a leaf,
oars: fanning wings.

LU CHI 200 CNSK 75.1040

Written in spring of 1208, Lu, eighty-four, at Shanyin.
"Orchid Inn" and "Plum Shop Bridge," both in Shanyin.

Village Living

On uplands facing me
they burn three-year-old fields,

and from a near creek
you can hear them haul water.

Ramshackle house rakes aft
but still is home;

and lean ox,
obsolete,
can still plough.

LU CHI 202 CNSK 78.1075

Lu, at eighty-four in Shanyin; wintertime.

Spring Mixed

Night, night, crackling firewood
bright against quilt;

at Mount Yu one measure of rice,
thousand coins.

Me, old farmhand,
can't shoulder this blame—

highway's stream of poor
forever shakes my heart.

LU CHI 204 CNSK 81.1103

144

Written in 1209, Lu, eighty-five, in Shanyin.
"Mount Yu" is in Chekiang.

As Things Are

On belevedere, against rail,
gaze into far vault:

sky's Silver Stream flows athwart
Big Dipper and Herd-Boy.

Another year's war drums,
trumpet: Elm Frontier Road—

riding my horse, I peered
at these same stars.

LU CHI 204 CNSK 83.1126

1109, Lu, eighty-five, in Shanyin.
   "Big Dipper" and "Herd-Boy" are both constellations. Compare:
Ἄρκτον Θ᾽, ἥν καὶ Ἅμαξαν ἐπίκλησιν καλέουσιν, "the Bear which
people also call the Wain." (Od.v.273)
   "Elm Frontier Road" is in Hopei.
   "Sky's Silver Stream" is the Milky Way.

Sigh from a Book

Last locusts have cleared out:
we frolic in fall harvest;

throngs of sheaves brought to
threshing floor. Rain stopped: bright.

They hide smiles,
thinking the old guy doesn't twig:

but I still prize infinite
miles of Jade Frontier.

Rain, night, lone boat, I
sleep on Mirror Lake;

autumn's wind's thrummed strings
fill marsh bulrush.

Writer has tears;
the kind you can't brush aside:

to see homeland's ninefold luck
as before foe came.

LU CHI 205 CNSK 83.1132

Written in the autumn of 1209, Lu eighty-five, in Shanyin.
"Jade Frontier" in the northwestern part of China.
"Mirror Lake" in Shanyin.
"To see homeland's" is literally: "seeks to see map of nine parts as it was during 1008 to 1016, i.e., before the Juchens invaded."

Design by David Bullen
Typeset in Mergenthaler Sabon
by Wilsted & Taylor
Printed by Thomson-Shore
on acid-free paper